D1072130

A Study of "Monarchical" Tendencies in the United States from 1776 to 1801

Reprints in Government and Political Science

Editor-in-Chief: Richard H. Leach
DUKE UNIVERSITY

A STUDY OF "MONARCHICAL" TENDENCIES IN THE UNITED STATES FROM 1776 TO 1801

By LOUISE BURNHAM DUNBAR

With a New Preface by the Author

Johnson Reprint Corporation

New York and London

1970

The edition reproduced here was originally
published in 1922, © 1923

Library of Congress Catalog Card Number: 71-111389

Printed in the U. S. A.

PREFACE

The Preface to the original edition of this study (on p. 7) states briefly how I had undertaken to contribute to a fuller and clearer understanding of the subject. I should have added that the book is more than a compilation. Each episode or situation is scrutinized with sufficient care to stimulate readers to form their own opinions as to its credibility and its part in our country's transition from dependent Colonies to independent States and—after some painful experimentation—a potentially powerful Nation by 1801.

"Monarchical" Tendencies was published in 1922 as No. 1 of Vol. X of the University of Illinois Studies in the Social Sciences. It was widely circulated among subscribers to that series. After a slow start it gained recognition and was cited and quoted by numerous distinguished writers. In 1939 it was commended by Robert A. East, one of the contributors to *The Era of the American Revolution* (edited by Richard B. Morris, Columbia University Press), as a "judicious study of a highly important and difficult subject." (Robert East is himself an authority on this as it relates to "The Massachusetts Conservatives in the Critical Period.") More recently it has been cited in *The Reinterpretation of Early American History*, edited by Ray A. Billington and written by specialists in our Colonial Period (The Huntington Library, San Marino, California, 1966).

Splendid new editions of the writings of the Founding Fathers are now becoming available. I believe they will confirm my findings on "monarchical" tendencies. My research for a volume on "The Royal Governors of British North America from the Mid-eighteenth Century to 1776," which I have well under way, is proving to be in harmony with my "monarchical" findings.

The 200th anniversary of the American Declaration of Independence is less than ten years in the future. The bicentennial of the framing of the Constitution of 1787 will be observed eleven years later. Such special occasions (and the celebrations which precede them) can gain new dimensions if the "monarchical" predilections and projects which complicated decision making in the last quarter of the eighteenth century—although for the most part overcome—are better known and understood.

Louise Burnham Dunbar
November 29, 1969

UNIVERSITY OF ILLINOIS STUDIES
IN THE
SOCIAL SCIENCES

Vol. X March, 1922 No. 1

Published by the University of Illinois
Under the Auspices of the Graduate School
Urbana, Illinois

A Study of "Monarchical" Tendencies in the United States from 1776 to 1801

BY

LOUISE BURNHAM DUNBAR, Ph.D.

Instructor in History
University of Illinois

CONTENTS

PREFACE

The present study is an attempt to add something of value and interest to the understanding of the nature, causes, and extent, as well as the evidences and influence of monarchical tendencies in the United States from 1776 to 1801. Many writers have touched upon the subject. Some have disposed of it with a few sweeping generalizations; others have given considerable space to certain of the more striking manifestations of monarchical tendencies. I have prepared a study which presents, so far as I know them, all the more important data on which justifiable generalizations can be based. By its relative completeness and by its arrangement of the facts, for the most part, in chronological order, this study should afford an account somewhat clearer and more comprehensive than those attempted in preceding treatments.

Foremost among numerous persons to whom I am indebted for valuable criticism and suggestions are Professor Theodore C. Pease and Professor Evarts B. Greene, of the University of Illinois. The latter assisted in an advisory capacity from the very outset of the work. Any errors in respect to fact or treatment are, of course, entirely my own.

CHAPTER I

ATTITUDE OF THE AMERICANS TOWARDS KINGSHIP ON THE EVE OF THE REVOLUTION

In 1765 the Stamp Act Congress professed to be "sincerely devoted, with the warmest sentiments of affection and duty to his Majesty's person and government," and "inviolably attached to the present happy establishment of the Protestant succession."[1] In the closing paragraph of the Resolutions of the Congress George III is called "the best of sovereigns,"[2] and four days later, in a similar document, the members declared, "We glory in being the subjects of the best of kings."[3] Assertions of this sort, often repeated in the immediately succeeding years, ill accord with the famous indictment of the King in the Declaration of Independence.[4] The contrast is more or less evident in almost any historical treatment of the ten years prior to the Revolutionary War. The development of this hostility to King George and its extension to the very institution of kingship demands attention at the outset of our investigation.

Throughout the Stamp Act controversy, despite the high pitch of popular indignation,[5] the Americans accorded respect to the King and cast the blame upon his ministers.[6] Just as attention

[1]William Macdonald, *Select Charters and other Documents Illustrative of American History, 1606–1775*, 314.

[2]*Ibid.*, 315.

[3]H. Niles, *Principles and Acts of the Revolution*, Petition to the House of Commons, 459.

[4]*Journals of the Continental Congress*, V, 511-514.

[5]For transcripts of official reports on the intensity of feeling see letters of Nov. 4, 5, 8, 1765, by General Gage, *American Stamp Act Collection*, Bancroft transcript, Manuscripts Division, Library of Congress. For secondary account see that by G. E. Howard, *Preliminaries of the Revolution* (*The American Nation: A History*, VIII), ch. VIII.

[6]Jeremy Belknap comments on absence of disrespect to the King as illustrated by letters and papers passing between "the Sons of Liberty in Portsmouth and their brethren in Boston, Providence, Connecticut, New York, &c., during the time of the Stamp Act." Belknap Papers, I, 120-121 (*Massachusetts Historical Society*

centered upon the ministry as the hated oppressor, so attention centered upon the King as the source of deliverance and his part in the repeal was emphasized and exalted. In taking this attitude the Americans were probably influenced by the English newspaper account, which arrived on the same ship with the official dispatch. This described the King's participation in a truly impressive manner. For example, it declared that as he had gone through the streets on his way to the House of Lords to give his assent to the repeal, "there was such a vast Concourse of People, huzzaing, clapping Hands, &c. that it was several Hours before his Majesty reached the House."[7] A diary entry expressed the general sentiment when it recorded the arrival of "the glorious news of the total repeal of the Stamp Act, which was signed by his Majesty King George the 3d of ever glorious memory, which God long preserve and his illustrious house."[8]

Again, the King was made the central figure in the jubilant celebrations of the event in America. Emblematical paintings were prepared in some places, box-like arrangements set one above another. Upon these the King was depicted in all his glory— and in model company! The upper compartment of the Boston pyramid was decorated by "heads of King and Queen & fourteen of ye Patriots, being four on a side."[9] That at Newport was still more splendid. "In the Centre of the third, [highest compartment] his Majesty in his Royal Robes sat enthroned, & with a most gracious Aspect, pointed to a Scroll . . . inscribed in Capitals, 'Stamp Act Repealed 1766, G. R.'" Pitt, with Magna

Collections, 5th ser., II). A vivid account of the demonstrations against the ministry is contained in "An anonymous diary of Events in America" [by Ebenezer Hazard], Feb. 7, 1765, to June 30, 1770," *American Stamp Act Collection*, Manuscripts Division, Library of Congress. The famous incident of Patrick Henry's speech and the interrupting cries of "Treason" is told by himself in his *Life and Correspondence and Speeches* I, 81. See also Howard, *Preliminaries of the Revolution*, 144. Compare *American Historical Review*, XXVI, 727-729, 745.

[7]Reprinted in America in handbill form. For facsimile see J. Winsor, *Narrative and Critical History of America*, VI, 33.

[8]Diary of John Rowe, *Massachusetts Historical Society Proceedings*, 2d ser., X, 62.

[9]P. 41, Stevens, Transcript of Hazard's narrative for 1765-1770, *Stamp Act Congress*, Manuscripts Division, Library of Congress.

Charta, was at the right of the King, while Camden, with the Bill of Rights, completed this interesting group.[10]

The above passages have been quoted not because they are quaint and amusing but because they indicate one of the most important features of the theory of kingship held by the American colonists.[11] The wearer of the crown was expected to be the champion of the rights of his people and accordingly was the center of popular interest in government.[12] If he should fail so much the worse for him, but the people would be slow to admit failure. Thus every year till after the bloodshed at Lexington and Concord there were expressions by Americans of loyalty to the King,[13]

[10]For other celebrations see Stevens, *op. cit.*, June, 1766, and Rowe's *Diary*, May 19 and June 4, 1766, *op. cit.*, 62.

[11]A feature which has survived in the popular attitude towards the President, as depicted in an account like that by Gaillard Hunt, "The President of the United States;" *Wisconsin Historical Publications*, LXIII, 76-98.

[12]Of course, the writer means this to apply to national or imperial government rather than local.

[13]The references in the following cases are to issues of the *Newport Mercury* unless otherwise indicated. Most of the data is of a nature to have been also printed elsewhere and could be located by a person who did not have access to the *Mercury* but did have the other sources at hand. Some of the early issues of the *Mercury* carry two dates in their subtitle. In making citations below only the second is used. For example, the first reference is recorded as "*N. M.*, Jan. 12, 1767," rather than "*Newport Mercury*, from Monday, January 5, — to Monday, January 12, 1767."

Reply of the House of Burgesses to the Lieutenant Governor, Nov. 6, 1766, (*N. M.*, Jan. 12, 1767, p. 1).

Reply of the Massachusetts House of Representatives to the Governor, Jan. 31, 1767, (Feb. 9, 1767, p. 2).

Celebrations of first anniversary of Stamp Act repeal, (Rowe, *Diary*, in *Massachusetts Historical Society Proceedings*, 2d ser., X, 63; *N. M.*, Mar. 23, 1767, p. 1).

St. Patrick's Day feast in Boston, (Mar. 30, 1767, p. 1).

Article by "Liberus," (*ibid.*, p. 1).

Massachusetts Circular Letter, Feb. 11, 1768, (S. Adams, *Writings*, I, 188).

Petition to the Governor by the inhabitants of Boston, June 14, 1768, (*N. M.*, June 27, 1768, p. 2).

Instructions to representatives of the town of Boston, June 17, 1768, (June 27, 1768, p. 3).

Non-importation Agreement by New York merchants, Sept. 5, 1768, (Sept. 19, 1768, p. 3.)

Extra-legal Convention in Massachusetts, Sept. 26, 1768, (Oct. 3, 1768, p. 2).

Letter from London describing Dr. Franklin's activities, (Dec. 5, 1768, p. 2).

or rather to their theory of kingship, even though the last and perhaps most famous of these, the petition of Congress to the King July 8, 1775, was in a sense an ultimatum to King George.[14]

Loyalty waned but slowly despite the fact that the months and

Report in South Carolina Assembly, Nov. 18 (?), 1768, (Jan. 9, 1769, p. 1).
Resolutions in the Georgia Assembly, Dec. 24, 1768, (Jan. 30, 1769, p. 4).
Petitions of the Pennsylvania Assembly, Sept. 22, 1768, (Feb. 27, 1769, p. 1).
Instructions of the Town of Boston, May 8, 1769, (May 22, 1769, p. 2).
Resolves of House of Burgesses, May 16, 1679, (June 12, 1769, p. 1).
Celebrations of King's birthday, June 4, 1770, (Rowe, *Diary*, *op. cit.*, 75).
Address of Council of Massachusetts, Mar. 20, 1770, (*N. M.*, Apr. 2, 1770, p. 1).
Address to the King by "Sidney," from the *Parliamentary Spy*, (Apr. 23, 1770, pp. 1-2). Note how conspicuous a place is given to this reprint.
Complaint of House of Representatives of Massachusetts against Governor Bernard, (May 14, 1770, p. 2).
Message from Massachusetts House of Representatives to Lieutenant-Governor, Oct. 13, 1770, (Oct. 29, 1770, p. 2).
Celebration of Queen's birthday, Jan. 18, 1771, (Rowe, *Diary*, *op. cit.*, 77.)
Virginia Petition to the King, (*N. M.*, Feb. 25, 1771, p. 1).
Reprint from *Poor Richard's Almanac* for the year 1758, (Mar. 6, 1771, p. 2).
Address by Massachusetts House of Representatives to the Governor, Apr. 24, 1771, (S. Adams, *Writings*, II, 168–169).
Article by "Candidus," in *Boston Gazette*, Sept. 16, 1771. (S. Adams, *Writings*, II, 220).
Celebration of King's birthday, June 4, 1772, (Rowe, *Diary*, *op cit.*, 78).
Items relating to royal household, (*N. M.*, Apr. 20, 1772, p. 1; Apr. 27, p. 2; *Supplement*, Apr. 27, p. 1).
Celebrations of King's birthday and coronation anniversary, 1773, (Rowe, *Diary*, *op. cit.*, 79).
Debates of the First Continental Congress, as recorded, contain no evidence of hostility to king or monarchy. (*Journals*, I; J. Adams' notes and account, *Works*, II, 365-401). For expressions favorable to monarchy see *Journals*, I, 82, 86.
Petition to the King by First Continental Congress, Oct., 1774, (*ibid.*, I, 53, 115–121).
Celebration at first appearance of the Newport Light-Infantry, (*N. M.* Apr. 17, 1775, p. 3).
Address of North Carolina Assembly to Governor, Apr. 7 (?), 1775, (May 1, 1775, p. 1).
Letter from New York Committee of Association to Mayor of London, May 15, 1775, (June 5, 1775, p. 1).
Letter from New York Provincial Congress to the people of Quebec, June 2, 1775, (June 19, 1775, p. 2).
Correspondence between New York Provincial Congress and General Washington, June 26, 1775, (July 10, 1775, p. 3).
Second Petition of Congress to the King, July 8, 1775, (*Journals*, II, 158-161).

[14] J. Adams, *Works*, II, 410-411.

years had passed without the expected interposition by the King in behalf of the colonists. By 1771 a writer so widely read as "Candidus" was declaring that the only effect of loyal petitions had been to bring new burdens upon the Americans.[15] But reproach was not at first directed against the King but rather against the ministry,[16] the Parliament, and even the English people. To be sure, the precedent of the tyranny of Charles I was cited in opposition to the quartering of royal troops in America.[17] Yet Samuel Adams cited the "unspotted loyalty" of the colonies as an argument against the necessity of the act. He placed express reliance upon the "wisdom and goodness of his present Majesty" and feared only a possible future tyrant.[18]

Down to 1769 and 1770 American writers often lauded the British King and constitution in the same breath in which they denounced the ministry.[19] They directed much of the brunt of their attack against the royal representatives in the colonies rather than against royalty.[20] They cast the blame upon Parlia-

[15] S. Adams, *Writings*, II, 282.

[16] For an expression of this reproach by John Adams see his *Works*, X, 246.

[17] By "Antoninus" in the *Boston Evening Post*, quoted in the *Newport Mercury*, Mar. 2, 1767, p. 1.

[18] S. Adams in the *Boston Gazette*, Dec. 26, 1768, *Writings*, I, 277, 275.

[19] "Right, Wrong, and Reasonable, with regard to America," *Newport Mercury*, Aug. 3, 1767, pp. 2-3.

Reprint of "Sidney's" address to the King, Dec. 19, 1769, *ibid*, Apr. 23, 1770, pp. 1-2.

An inflammatory address against Lord North is found in the *Supplement* to the *Newport Mercury*, Aug. 8, 1774, p. 1.

Letter from Samuel Stillmen to Patience Wright, Boston, Nov. 13, 1774, *Massachusetts Historical Society Proceedings*, 3d ser., X, 475.

Comment by Thomas Paine, *Political Writings*, I, 169-170, quoted by Tyler, *Literary History of the American Revolution*, I, 457.

Lines copied from "a London Paper," *Newport Mercury*, July 3, 1775, p. 4.

See also letter from New York provincial congress to the people of Quebec, June 2, 1775, *ibid.*, June 19, 1775, p. 2.

[20] Letter from the *Boston Gazette*, Sept. 28, 1772, *ibid.*, Oct. 5, 1772, p. 2.

Report that Edmund Burke had blamed colonial governors for the troubles, *ibid.*, May 16, 1774, p. 1.

Account of the burning in effigy of Hutchinson at Philadelphia, May 3, 1774, *ibid.*, May 16, 1774, p. 2.

See also John Adams, *Works*, X, 246, 454, 479.

ment[21] and even upon the English people[22] in a way which more or less exempted the King.

Nevertheless, during the two years just mentioned, American opposition to Government measures gained new force and confidence.[23] One manifestation of this change was to be found in certain attacks upon the King himself. He was most disrespectfully ridiculed as the "noodle to an old woman."[24] The wish was expressed that "three quarters of the nation had not reason to think" that certain lines upon the obstinate Agamemnon were "very applicable at this present time:"

> "That you are honest, we are sure,
> Yet, if you give to rascals power,
> The wrongs you suffer them to do,
> Will all be justly laid on you."[25]

The loyal addresses to the King were now parodied, as appears from an address "To his Sublime Majesty Oknookortunkogog" who is praised for his loving consideration for his people manifested in his "late order for the destruction of the poisonous weed tea."[26]

[21]Address to the people of England in *Boston Gazette*, Sept. 21, 1767, *Newport Mercury*, Sept. 28, 1767, p. 1.

Address of New York Assembly to Governor, Nov. 23, 1767, *ibid.*, Dec. 7, 1767, p. 2.

Article from the *Public Ledger*, Apr. 29, 1774, *Newport Mercury*, Aug. 15, 1774, p. 1.

Virginia's instructions to deputies to Congress, Aug. 1-6, 1774, *ibid.*, Sept. 5, 1774, p. 2.

Hall, *History of Eastern Vermont*, 199. (Resolutions of "eighteen delegates from twelve towns," Oct. 20, 1774.)

[22]Letters to *Boston Gazette*, Aug. 31 and Sept. 14, *Newport Mercury*, Sept. 7 and 21, 1767, pp. 2, 1, respectively.

Roger Martyn to the *Boston Gazette*, *Newport Mercury*, Sept. 21, 1767, pp. 1-2.

Note, on the other hand, the tendency to make common cause with the English people as shown by the large place given to the John Wilkes controversy (in the *Newport Mercury*, during 1769 and the first weeks of 1770), and such an address as that in the *Boston Gazette*, Sept. 21, 1767, *Newport Mercury*, Sept. 28, 1767, p. 1.

[23]For a convenient summary see J. S. Bassett, *Short History of the United States*, 171–174.

[24]This refers, of course, to his deference to the dowager Queen. See *Newport Mercury*, Oct. 30, 1769, p. 1.

[25]*Ibid.*

[26]From the *Massachusetts Spy*. His Majesty's answer is also recorded in the usual ceremonious style. *Newport Mercury*, Apr. 11, 1774, p. 2. A similar satire

One of the "Letters of Junius," appearing in America early in 1770, contained a very explicit account of monarchical ideas in the colonies.[27] Whatever his identity, "Junius" was undoubtedly one of the most effective political writers of all time [28] and was widely read in America.[29] The passage in question will speak for itself.

"They [the colonies] were ready enough to distinguish between you [the King] and your Ministers. They complained of an Act of the Legislature, but traced the Origin of it no higher than to the Servants of the C - n: They pleased themselves with the Hope that their S-r-n, if not favourable to their Cause, at least was impartial. The decisive, personal Part you took against them, has effectually banished that first Distinction from their Minds. They consider you as united with your Servants against A-r-a, and know how to distinguish the S-r-n and a venal P-t on one Side, from the real Sentiments of the English People on the other. Looking forward to Independence, they might possibly receive you for their K-g; but, if ever you retire to A-r-a, be assured they will give you such a Covenant to digest, as the Presbytery of Scotland would have been ashamed to offer to Charles the Second. They left their native Land in Search of Freedom, and found it in a Desart. Divided as they are into a Thousand Forms of Policy and Religion, there is one Point in which they all agree: They equally detest the Pageantry of a K-g, and the supercilious Hypocrisy of a Bishop."[30]

In respect to his influence on public opinion "Junius" was a fore-

is found in what purported to be a Salem item regarding the coronation anniversary of George III, *ibid.*, Oct. 12, 1772, p. 3.

[27]The letter of Dec. 16, 1769, directed to the King. Printed in the *Newport Mercury*, Feb. 19, 1770, pp. 1-3.

[28]On the identity of "Junius" and his superiority over other writers of political invective see *Encyclopaedia Britannica*, XV, 558.

If, perchance, "Junius" was Thomas Pownall, as is claimed by the biographer of the latter, the account is even more interesting to the present study than already indicated, for Pownall had spent years in America and was a serious student of its affairs. See *Life of Thomas Pownall* by C. A. W. Pownall, chapter XII. See also the *Literature of American History* (Larned ed.), 873, for an estimate of Pownall's book on colonial government.

[29]"The paper signed JUNIUS, which has been published in Boston, Rhode-Island, Philadelphia and this city, has also been re-printed in the South-Carolina Gazette of the 19th of February last, from the St. James's Chronicle of December the 21st". *Newport Mercury*, Mar. 19, 1770, p. 3.

[30]*Ibid.*, Feb. 19, 1770, p. 2.

runner of Thomas Paine. Unlike the later writer, however, "Junius" did not attack monarchical institutions as such. He painted in glowing colors the happy days at the opening of the reign of George III, and asked no more of him than that he should "distinguish between the conduct, which becomes the permanent dignity of a K-g, and that which serves only to promote the temporary interest and miserable ambition of a Minister."[31] He had only praise for the readiness of men "to sacrifice their lives to save a good Prince, or to oppose a bad one."[32] He believed the character of the English people a sufficient safeguard against the tyrannical attempts of any English king.

Another indication that the censure of a king did not necessarily involve the censure of kingship is found in the expressed hope that King George might yet mend his ways. "A Chronological Table of Epithets" for British rulers, ranging from "The Glorious" to "The Never Right," suspended judgment in the case of George by leaving a blank space opposite his name.[33] The fable of "The Lion and the Fox" contained these lines:

"May gracious Kings have all the Rev'rence due,
And ev'ry Stuart find his Cromwell too."[34]

As late as July 3, 1775, the following verse appeared:

"In time be wise, drive Traitors from thy breast,
And let the just, the honest round thee move;
So shall the sinking State once more be blest
And thou be happy in thy people's love."[35]

But, in addition to the attacks upon the King, already discussed, there were attacks upon the monarchical institution. An early and apparently isolated one appeared in the summer of 1768

[31] *Newport Mercury*, Feb. 19, 1770, p. 1.

[32] This expression is from a letter appearing later in 1770, in *ibid.*, June 11, 1770, p. 1. For further attacks against the King rather than against the kingship see the taunts of the "Whisperer" (*ibid.*, July 23, 1770, p. 1), the "Description of a Tory" (*ibid.*, Sept. 2, 1771, p. 4), a Junius letter (*ibid.*, Sept. 30, 1771, p. 1), comments by "Candidus" (Samuel Adams, *Writings*, II, 252, 262, 273, 292–293), extract from letter from London (*Newport Mercury*, Apr. 27, 1772, *Supplement*, p. 1), verses quoted from the *North Briton* (*ibid.*, July 13, 1772, p. 2).

[33] *Newport Mercury*, Oct. 30, 1769, p. 2.

[34] *Ibid.*, Nov. 2, 1772, p. 1.

[35] Copied from "a London Paper," by the *Newport Mercury* of July 3, 1775, p. 4. The title is significant, "An Elegy to the Memory of the best of Kings."

in an appeal by "A Son of Liberty"[36] to the "Pennsylvania Farmer" to leave the "temporizers" in Philadelphia and unite with Mr. Otis. The latter is praised for his "*firm* and *manly* spirit" which "fears neither *commissioners*, *generals*, *armies*, nor *navies*, but, inspired with the eminations of arch [word nearly obliterated][37] *antimonarchical principles*, . . . rouses the inhabitants and heroically alienates their affection from *Kingly* and British *subordination*."[38]

A more characteristic attack on kingship was expressed in an article from the "North-Briton" reprinted in America in 1769. This subjected the King's speech of recent date to a most scathing criticism and cited the "fatal effects" upon popular opinion of a speech by King Charles in 1628. At the same time it professed to be criticising the ministry, not the King, by quoting the "maxim in the English constitution *that the king can do no wrong*." The general effect was to expose the absurdity of the maxim cited.[39] An account, imbued with hostility to the institution of kingship, traced the development of British monarchy from the time of its introduction by "tyrannical Anglo-Saxon invaders." It called attention to repeated encroachments of the King and nobles upon the liberties of the people, and told of the happy success of the Italian cities in overthrowing their "haughty lords" and putting the power into the hands of the people.[40] Some writers, however, were not content with citing the tyranny of the Stuarts and its results for King Charles, but vigorously attacked or ridiculed members of the succeeding line of rulers.[41] On the other

[36]"To J-H-N D-ck-n-s-n Esq." See below, page 19.

[37]Both appearance and context suggest "arch."

[38]Letter to the *Pennsylvania Chronicle* headed "Boston, June-1768," *Newport Mercury*, Aug. 15, 1768, p. 2. Contrast with letter of July 18, 1768, signed by James Otis and reprinted from the *Political Register*, *Newport Mercury*, Apr. 17, 1769, p. 1. For an interpretation see Tyler, *Literary History of the American Revolution*, I, 43.

[39]*Newport Mercury*, Aug. 21, 1769, p. 4. Apparently the colonists, except some of ultra aristocratic and "High Church" proclivities, did not regard a king as a sacred personage. For an article along these lines see C. H. Van Tyne, "Influence of the Clergy, and of Religious and Sectarian Forces, on the American Revolution," *American Historical Review*, XIX, 44-64. The footnote references as well as the text are very helpful to an understanding of the situation.

[40]Reprinted from the *Royal Magazine* by the *Newport Mercury*, Mar. 5, 1770, p. 1.

[41]Article from the *St. James's Chronicle* reprinted in the *Newport Mercury*, Sept.

hand, one part of the British theory of monarchy could be, and actually was, acclaimed by opponents of its other features, namely, that the relation between King and subjects was purely contractual and dissolved by the tyranny of the former.[42] As will be noted a little later this idea was the basis of the Declaration of Independence.[43]

It is natural that the American attitude towards kings other than their own should have influenced their general conception of monarchical government. Thus examples of tyrannical rule, from antiquity to the time of writing, were cited early in 1767. Absolutism in Spain was deplored and a scathing reference made to "Prussia . . . as absolute as any monarch of the East." This attack was not, however, directed against monarchical institutions in general but against the dangerous employment of the soldiery.[44] A "Political Picture of Europe, for June, 1770" was published in an American paper. It is more antimonarchical in character and of considerable interest, especially since its brevity and humorous cast must have attracted the attention of any reader of the issue in which it appeared. A few quotations will indicate the character of this list of contemporary sovereigns:

"The French King leading Monarchs by the nose; the political Puppet-master of Europe."

"The King of Prussia, a fox in a bramble-bush; peeping first out at one corner, and then at another; but seeing an old woman watching him, whips in his head and sits still."

"The King of Poland a Monarch without a crown, wandering through a court, without Nobles."

"The Grand Seignior stretched in a melancholy posture on the borders of the Black Sea, half covered with ooze and seaweeds."

The dozen other rulers described fared little better in this account. The British King, at the end of the list, was pictured as "much puzzled; a fading Rose and a broken Trident lying at his feet."[45]

7, 1772, p. 2., and article from the *Gentleman's Magazine*, *ibid.*, Feb. 8, 1773, p. 3.

[42] See especially "Extract of a Letter to the King, inserted in the London Evening Post, of Aug. 22, 1772," reprinted in the *Newport Mercury*, Nov. 9, 1772, pp. 2-3. The idea will be found in many of the attacks on the king already cited.

[43] See below, p. 21, footnote 65.

[44] "Antoninus", quoted in the *Newport Mercury*, Mar. 2, 1767, p. 1. He was opposing the quartering of soldiers upon the population. See above, p. 13.

[45] *Newport Mercury*, Oct. 1, 1770, p. 2.

Far abler than the antimonarchical writings just considered were three defences of kingship, contained respectively in the publications of the "Pennsylvania Farmer," the "Westchester Farmer," and "The Farmer Refuted." Their wide circulation and popularity are well known, and their influence unquestioned. The writers supported kingship, whatever their other views might be. The first[46] expressly approved the overthrow of the Stuarts as improving the condition of the English people. But he considered it no precedent for a revolt by the colonists, for, he said, "if once we are separated from our mother country, what new form of government shall we adopt. . . . Torn from the body, to which we are united by religion, liberty, laws, affections, relations, language and commerce, we must bleed at every vein."[47] He felt sure of the general existence of loyalty to the King[48] yet he betrayed a dread that if the oppressive policy of government were not reversed popular opinion would be aroused against even the legal powers of the crown, as in the days of Charles I, and monarchy be again overthrown.[49]

The "Westchester Farmer"[50] appeared upon the scene a few weeks after the closing of the Continental Congress of 1774.[51] Ablest of Loyalist writers, and equalled "for immediate effect upon the mass of readers" by no one, perhaps, but Thomas Paine,[52] his utterances on monarchy compel our attention. His best known remark on the point, so far as present day readers are concerned, is probably his exclamation, " . . . if I must be enslaved, let it be by a KING at least, and not by a parcel of upstart, lawless committeemen."[53] In addition he denounced as heresy the theory advanced by the Continental Congress that

[46]Writing in 1768. See *Writings of John Dickinson* (P. L. Ford, ed.), *Memoirs of the Historical Society of Pennsylvania*, XIV, 277-406.

It will be remembered that Dickinson also composed the "Declaration of Rights," of the Stamp Act Congress, the popular "Liberty Song," the "Olive Branch Petition," and other important papers.

[47]*Ibid.*, 326.

[48]*Ibid.*, 350

[49]See also *ibid.*, pp. 387-388.

[50]The Reverend Samuel Seabury, as is well known.

[51]Namely, Nov. 16, 1774, Tyler, *Literary History of the American Revolution*, I, 342.

[52]*Ibid.*,348-349.

[53]*Ibid.*, 340.

American allegiance was due only to the King and not to Parliament, a doctrine he believed meant to pave the way to sedition.[54] On the contrary, the King held his position by act of Parliament, therefore to disown the authority of Parliament was virtually to renounce the King,[55] which would lead to the tyranny of Congress, the only tyranny Americans just then needed to fear.[56]

With a hundred and thirty years of successful republican existence behind us, it is difficult to conceive that men could ever have expected an independent "United States" to adopt a different government. But listen to the "Westchester Farmer," in 1774. In case of successful rebellion against England, "Probably it would cost the blood of a great part of the inhabitants of America to determine what kind of government we should have, whether a monarchy or a republic. Another effusion of blood would be necessary to fix a monarch, or to establish a commonwealth."[57]

Still more important is the fact that the able refutations[58] of the "Westchester Farmer," penned by the youthful Alexander Hamilton, upheld monarchical government and the ruling house. This is best illustrated by part of a paragraph near the close of "The Farmer Refuted," namely: "I earnestly lament the unnatural quarrel between the parent state and the colonies, and most ardently wish for a speedy reconciliation—a perpetual and *mutually* beneficial union. . . . I am a warm advocate for limited monarchy, and an unfeigned well-wisher to the present Royal Family."[59] By limited monarchy Hamilton meant exactly what the words say, and not a balance of monarchy, aristocracy, and democracy as the definition was so often made. He wrote, "Perhaps, indeed, it may with propriety be said that the king is the only sovereign of the empire. The part which the people have in the legislature may more justly be considered as a limitation of

[54] A "gilding with which they have enclosed the pill of sedition, to entice the unwary colonists to swallow it the more readily down." Tyler, *op. cit.*, 343.

[55] *Ibid.*, 343.

[56] The "Congress Canvassed," as quoted in Tyler, *op. cit.*, 343.

[57] *Ibid.*, 26-27, as quoted in Tyler, *op. cit.*, 344.

[58] "A Full Vindication of the Measures of Congress . . . in answer to a letter . . . of a Westchester Farmer," Hamilton, *Works* (Lodge ed.), I, 1-50, and "The Farmer Refuted," *ibid.*, 51-169. The former appeared late in 1774, the latter early in 1775. Tyler, *op. cit.*, I, 384-385. For other passages than that quoted bearing on the subject see Hamilton, *Works*, I, 8-9, 64, 76, 78.

[59] *Ibid*, 168.

the sovereign authority, to prevent its being exercised in an oppressive and despotic way."[60] All he was asking for the colonists was a due share in this system of limitation.

Thomas Paine's "Common Sense,"[61] the greatest literary factor working for independence in the first half of 1776, was throughout a scathing attack upon monarchical government. Its second part,[62] "Of Monarchy and Hereditary Succession," concentrated all of Paine's powers of sarcasm and ridicule upon this one subject.[63] The origin of kingship was in heathenism, its adoption by the Hebrews was by no divine guidance—quite the contrary—the hereditary principle associated with kingship had generally inflicted stupid rulers upon mankind. As to the peculiar excellence claimed for the British type of monarchy, it was contrary to reason, for, "The nearer any government approaches to a Republic, the less business there is for a King," and the greater waste in supporting such a figurehead! Paine, unintentionally no doubt, left a loophole for the erection of an elective monarchy, which might furnish later encouragement to men interested in the possibility of such a form in America. There may have been other patriot leaders than John Adams in 1776 who, secretly at least, scorned the writings of Paine.[64] But its unequalled popularity proved that the general public was ready at that time to oppose not only King George but also the institution which he represented.

The Declaration of Independence concentrated its attention upon King George and made no statement for or against monarchical institutions,[65] but the wholesale destruction of royal emblems[66]

[60]Hamilton, *Works*, I, 76.

[61]Published Jan. 10, 1776. *Writings of Thomas Paine* (Conway ed.), I, 67, footnote 1.

[62]Compare Richard Frothingham, *Rise of the Republic of the United States*, 472.

[63]"Common Sense" is printed in Paine's *Writings*, I, 69-120.

[64]That John Adams felt thus about Paine may be gathered from his comment, *Works*, II, 153. Perhaps, however, Paine's later career and a possible jealousy on the part of Adams as to originating the move for independence influenced the statement. See *ibid.*, II, 412.

[65]Perhaps this was sufficiently explained by the fact that the separation was legally based on the idea that George III had violated his contract with his American subjects, thereby absolving them from further allegiance. Compare *Writings and Speeches of Daniel Webster* (National ed.), I, 303-304; C. M. Walsh, *Political Science of John Adams*, 6. Compare and contrast C. H. Van Tyne, *The American Revolution* (*The American Nation: A History*, IX), 84-86.

[66]See Ezra Stiles, *Diary*, entry for Aug. 26, 1776, in transcript, Manuscripts

which followed bore witness to at least a momentary detestation of monarchy itself. The democratic constitutions adopted by the several states, as well as the absence of a strong central government, evidenced the persistence of this attitude. Yet traces remain of a preference for monarchy among the revolutionists. Some of these traces are indistinct and difficult to explain. For example, Joseph Warren in an oration at Boston had said, "But if these pacifick measures are ineffectual . . . you will . . . press forward until tyranny is trodden under foot; and you have fixed your adored Goddess, Liberty, fast by a *Brunswick's* side, on the *American* throne."[67] The figurative language would present no difficulties but for the phrase, "fast by a *Brunswick's* side," which suggests the orator was content to picture a continuance of some sort of monarchy in his country,[68] even one connected with the then ruling house.

In a somewhat similar vein was a letter written by John Adams in October, 1775. He touched upon the subject in so jocose a fashion as to leave one guessing his real attitude. Whatever he meant when he said that a plan for a "Continental King, . . . a Continental House of Lords, and a Continental House of Commons" was "whispered in the Coffee Houses"[69] he meant something different from the congressional government in force. Another letter by Adams contains the remark that "the colonies will have republics for their government, let us lawyers and your divine say what we will."[70] The "divine" referred to was Dr. Zubly

Division, Library of Congress. (Omitted from published diary.) A good brief account of the destruction of the Bowling Green statue of George III is in the *Massachusetts Historical Society Proceedings*, 2d ser., IV, 293-294. An exhaustive treatise on the use and destruction of royal emblems will be found in the same volume, 239-264.

[67]Oration, Mar. 6, 1775, to commemorate the Boston massacre. *American Archives*, 4th ser., II, 43.

[68]Contrast with statement in House of Lords, Nov. 10, 1775, that a gentlemen who was a large landowner in New England asserted "that the people of that Province were full of a levelling, republican spirit, which would never be rooted out till they . . . were compelled to bow under . . . constitutional Government . . . that . . . they were no less hostile against monarchical Government than against the rights of the British Parliament." *Ibid.*, 4th ser., VI, 134.

[69]To James Warren, Oct. 28, 1775, *Massachusetts Historical Society Collections*, LXXII, 167. Compare a letter to Mrs. Warren, Jan. 8, 1776, *ibid.*, 201-202, and her comment on it, Feb. 7, 1776, *ibid.*, 205-206.

[70]To Archibald Bullock, July 1, 1776, Adams, *Works*, IX, 414-415. The lines

of Georgia, a native of the Swiss Republic.[71] Although associated with the Loyalists after 1777 he was earlier on good terms with the revolutionists.[72] He had once said in the Second Continental Congress, "A republican government is little better than government of devils. I have been acquainted with it from six years old."[73] There is every reason to believe that he had supported his monarchical ideas in many a confidential talk with his colleagues in Congress.[74] In the letter quoted, Adams seemed to associate himself with Zubly in the matter. It is interesting to note that in his "Thoughts on Government" Adams left a loophole for a life tenure in the great offices of state. On the other hand, he characterized an important expression of monarchical views as "too absurd to be considered twice." On the whole the principles which Adams openly supported at the time were by no means monarchical.[75]

Still another defense of the monarchical principle on the eve of the Revolution was one under date of February 28, 1776, in which "Rationalis" addressed "To the Inhabitants of Pennsylvania" a refutation of the antimonarchical arguments of "Common Sense."[76] This address concerns us because its author professed, at least, to be willing to support independence as a last resort.[77] He used biblical citations to prove that monarchy was "not inconsistent with the Holy Scriptures" as claimed by "Common Sense." He declared that it was "as pleasing to the Almighty, if agreeable to the people, as any other form of Government"[78]. He next pointed out that republics had proved quite as turbulent as monarchies, giving concrete examples, both ancient and modern.[79] His conception of a monarchy was apparently based upon

quoted were to be repeated to Mr. Houston, who with Bullock and Zubly represented Georgia in the Second Continental Congress. See *ibid.*, II, 422.

[71] *Ibid.*, II, 421.

[72] *Biographical Congressional Directory*, 1136, and *National Cyclopaedia of American Biography*, III, 212.

[73] *Journals of the Continental Congress*, III, 491.

[74] Adams, *Works*, II, 423.

[75] See, for example, his letter to General Gates, *Works*, I, 207. See also Walsh, *Political Science of John Adams*, ch. II, "Early Democratic Views."

[76] *American Archives*, 4th ser., IV, 1527-1530.

[77] *Ibid.*, 1530. For loyalist refutations see Tyler, *op. cit.*, I, 479-481.

[78] *American Archives*, 4th ser., IV, 1529.

[79] *Ibid.*, 1529-1530.

contract,[80] yet he upheld the hereditary principle, using the "terrible disorders" of the elective monarchy of Poland as a warning against the non-hereditary type.[81] He also was bold enough to assert that England's own republican experiment had ended in the "absolute sway" of one man, Oliver Cromwell.[82]

"Rationalis" was met on his own ground by a disimpassioned address signed "Salus Populi."[83] The main feature in this argument was that it admitted the ill success of earlier republics but contended that America had unprecedented opportunities for success in the adoption of such a form. A somewhat similar article a few months later[84] emphasized the importance of entirely reforming American government, rather than "patching up" the old one, and said that "there must never be any power like a Kingly power" in America.[85] It declared against hereditary tenure on the ground that "wisdom is not a birthright," and against life tenure because "men's abilities and manners may change."[86]

On the other hand, an important expression of the monarchical views hinted at by Adams[87] has been preserved to us in an address which first appeared in the spring of 1776.[88] Carter Braxton, an aristocratic Virginian, a member of the Continental Congress, and a signer of the Declaration of Independence, was thought by

[80] *American Archives*, 4th ser., IV, 1529-1530.

[81] *Ibid.*, 1530.

[82] *Ibid.*, 1530.

[83] "To the People of North-America on the Different Kinds of Government," *ibid.*, 4 th ser., V, 180-183. Undated, but there placed under heading "March 1776."

[84] "The Interest of America," unsigned, *ibid.*, 4th ser., VI, 840-843. Classed with material for June, 1776.

[85] *Ibid.*, 842.

[86] *Ibid.*, 843.

[87] In his letter to James Warren, above, page 22.

[88] "Address to the Convention of the Colony and Ancient Dominion of Virginia, on the subject of Government in general, and recommending a particular form to their consideration. By a native of the Colony." Printed in *American Archives* 4th ser. VI, 748-754. Originally published in pamphlet form at Philadelphia and reprinted June 8, 1776, in the "*Virginia Gazette*" with a view to influencing the state constitutional convention. J. Adams, *Works*, IV, 202, editor's note.

some to be the author.[89] Patrick Henry called it a "silly thing"[90] and John Adams said it was "too absurd to be considered twice."[91] Henry admitted, however, that his "most esteemed republican form" of government had "many and powerful enemies" in Virginia.[92] It is difficult to judge how much sympathy the address in question aroused[93] among the "Barons of the South," as Adams termed the aristocratic Virginians.[94] It certainly produced little practical effect upon the Virginia constitution.[95] Yet its author seemed confident that his system was more truly adapted to the situation of America than the more purely democratic ones then advocated. Should the latter type be adopted, in the excitement of the moment, he felt sure it would not prove permanently satisfactory. As a result violent efforts would be made to restore the former system.[96] He praised the English constitution, perfected "by the vigilance, perseverance, and activity, of innumerable martyrs."[97] If any imperfections still remained they could be removed without the sacrifice of the entire structure. Former republican experiments were warnings rather than models.[98] After thus preparing the minds of his readers he unfolded before them a plan of state government in which the governor was elected by the representatives and held office "*during his good behaviour.*"[99] The other features of the plan were of a similar nature. As for a more general government it would seem he had nothing in mind but a Congress with rather extensive powers but with no single

[89]P. Henry to J. Adams, May 20, 1776, Adams, *Works*, IV, 201-202. Adams suggested it to be a "joint production of one native of Virginia, and two natives of New York." *Ibid.* IX, 387. For a brief account of Braxton see *Appletons' Cyclopaedia of American Biography* I, 361.

[90]Patrick Henry to John Adams, May 20, 1776, Adams, *Works*, IV, 201-202.

[91]*Ibid.*, IX, 387.

[92]*Ibid.*, IV, 201-202.

[93]At any rate, Braxton was a member of the first house of delegates under the new constitution. *Appletons' Cyclopaedia*, 361. For a New York connection see John Jay to Edward Rutledge, July 6, 1776, *American Archives*, 5th ser., I, 41.

[94]J. Adams, *Works*, I, 207; IX, 358, 388.

[95]See charts in Channing, *History of the United States*, III, 459-462.

[96]*American Archives*, 4th ser., VI, 749.

[97]*Ibid.*, 750.

[98]*Ibid.*, 751-752.

[99]*Ibid.*, 752-753. (The italics are not in the original.)

executive head.[100] As a whole, however, his pamphlet is of considerable significance to a study of "monarchical" tendencies in the period.

Apparently some fears were confessed in 1776 that there was "not publick virtue enough in the country" as basis for a republic.[101] Obviously the party in power generally discountenanced such fears. Thanks to the general trend of events and to the eloquent arguments of "Common Sense" republican enthusiasm rose high in 1776.[102] Yet the following passage, written near the end of that eventful year, is at least suggestive: "If I may be permitted, then, to deliver my opinion of the genius of the *Americans*. I shall say it is of a monarchical spirit; this is natural from the government they have ever lived under. It is therefore impossible to found a simple Republic in *America*. Another reason that operates very strongly against such a government is the great distinction of persons, and difference in their estates or property, which cooperates strongly with the genius of the people in favour of monarchy."[103]

This brings us to the end of the pre-revolutionary period. Monarchical institutions had become extremely unpopular. Antimonarchical forms of government were to have their trial. But if they were found wanting might not some men, remembering the seeming popularity of kingship in the earlier days, direct their efforts towards setting up an American kingship? Succeeding chapters of this study will answer this question in the affirmative.

[100]*American Archives*, 4th ser., VI, 753-754.

[101]See J. Adams to Mrs. Warren, Jan. 8, 1776, cited above p. 22, also S. McClintock to William Whipple, Greenland, N. H., Aug. 2, 1776. *American Archives*, 5th ser., I, 734.

[102]See above, pages 21-22.

[103]Signed "Farmer" and written at "Philadelphia, Nov. 5, 1776." *American Archives*, 5th ser., III, 518. The article concerned government for the individual states but seemed also applicable to a general government. Compare letter by a New Hampshire man (in same volume, p. 1226), written in December, 1776.

CHAPTER II

MONARCHICAL TENDENCIES IN THE UNITED STATES DURING THE REVOLUTIONARY WAR: THE PLAN OF COUNT DE BROGLIE

Thomas Jefferson once remarked parenthetically of certain American army officers that they were "trained to monarchy by military habits."[1] The utilization of the army as a basis for monarchical institutions was, indeed, the common factor in several propositions. The first of these was of French origin and centered around Charles François, Count de Broglie.[2] The count had been a trusted secret agent of Louis XV in that monarch's attempt to put a French prince on the Polish throne as well as in other projects. The prestige which he gained by his early successes in the Seven Years' War was somewhat impaired by his later misfortunes in that conflict. Circumstances conspiring against him, he was for some time a much neglected personage, so far as court favor and public employment were concerned. By the eve of the American Revolution his fortunes had improved, but hardly enough to satisfy a man of his character and previous career.[3] He seems to have been an inveterate enemy of England,[4] a great lover of glorious schemes,[5] and a man of much ambition.[6]

[1]Preface to "The Anas," Jefferson, *Writings* (Ford ed.), I, 157. Compare Colonel Nicola's assertion, below, 45. See also below, page 40.

[2]Born 1719, died 1781. For brief notices see *Encyclopaedia Britannica* (11th ed.), IV, 626; P. Larousse, *Grand Dictionnaire Universel Français*, IV, 1300; F. Kapp, *Life of John Kalb*, 80; H. Doniol, *Histoire de la Participation de la France à l'Établissement d'Amérique*, I, 636-637. A longer account is found in pp. 389-404 of an article by C. J. Stillé, "Comte de Broglie, the Proposed Stadtholder of America;" *Pennsylvania Magazine of History*, XI, 369-405.

[3]See Doniol, *op. cit.*, I, 636.

[4]See his "Mémoire" to Louis XVI, Doniol, *op. cit.*, II, 670-673, and, for English comments, Lord Stormont to Lord Weymouth, Feb. 6, 1777, B. F. Stevens, *Facsimiles of Manuscripts in European Archives Relating to America*, no. 1429.

[5]Such as securing the crown of Poland for a French prince (Stillé, *op. cit.*, 392–393), or sending an expedition to invade England, etc. (Doniol, *op. cit.*, II, 671-677). See also Kapp, *op. cit.*, 80.

[6]Doniol, *op. cit.*, II, 670; Kapp, *op. cit.*, 80, 93; Stillé, *op. cit.*, 389-391; *Deane Papers*, I, 429-431.

On November 5, 1776, the Count made two calls upon Silas Deane, American Agent at Paris. With him he brought Baron de Kalb,[7] a German in French service, who had toured America in 1768,[8] and wished to return there to aid the revolutionists. Kalb had been assistant quartermaster-general on Broglie's staff in the late war and had found in his superior officer a generous patron.[9] Thus it was natural that he was selected as chief assistant in the plan which Broglie had at heart, and was used to present it to Deane. There is double proof that this presentation was accomplished by or before December fifth. On that day Kalb wrote to the Count reporting "good progress"[10] and on the next Deane wrote to the Secret Committee of Congress as follows:[11] "I submit one thought to you: Whether if you could engage a great general of the highest character in Europe, such, for instance, as Prince Ferdinand, Marshal Broglio,[12] or others of equal rank to take the lead of your armies, whether such a step would not be politic, as it would give a character and credit to your military and strike perhaps a greater panic in our enemies. I only suggest the thought and leave you to confer with the Baron de Kalb on the subject at large."[13] The specific proposition, as stated a few days later, centered about the suggested installation of Broglie as generalissimo of the American forces, with absolute military powers, and, perhaps, some civil authority. He was to be subordinate to Congress and to hold his position for no more than three years.

The plan and its a ttendant circumstances make a strong appeal

[7]*Deane Papers* (*New York Historical Society Collections*, XIX-XXII), I, 342.

[8]*Ibid.*, I, 342; Kapp, *op. cit.*, 50-51, 68.

[9]Kapp, *op. cit.*, 38, 79-80.

[10]This report was acknowledged by Broglie in a letter quoted by Kapp, *op. cit.*, 94.

[11]*Deane Papers*, I, 404-405; F. Wharton, *Diplomatic Correspondence of the United States*, 392; etc. A short treatise on the affair, containing a number of quotations from the original correspondence, is found in Wharton, *op. cit.*, 392-396.

[12]The editor of the *Deane Papers* comments, "Deane confounds the Count Broglio with his brother, the Marshal and Duke," I, 404, n.

[13]See letter from Broglie to Kalb, December 11, 1776, and enclosure by Kalb, in a letter to Deane six days later, Kapp, *op. cit.*, 94-97; also in Doniol, *op. cit.*, the chapter, "Le Stathoudérat du Comte de Broglie;" II, 50-84, especially 62-74. For the enclosure mentioned see *Deane Papers*, I, 427-431; Stevens, *Facsimiles*, no. 604.

to the imagination and tempt one to unlimited conjecture. For instance, it is quite conceivable that Count Broglie's previous endeavors to set a French prince on the Polish throne[14] suggested the idea of an elective monarchy for America. Broglie had in mind a man of the rank of "the Prince of Nassau" (stadtholder in the Netherlands) as meeting the requirements for his American generalissimo.[15] If an elective monarchy should be installed the generalissimo would enjoy an unrivalled opportunity to win the "election." But with no actual proof of such ulterior motives it is more profitable to consider the potentialities of the plan itself and the impression it probably made upon those who knew of its existence.

America's supreme need for a leader who could unite factions, attract a brave and efficient personal following, and order all things by his own power,[16] justified to Broglie the granting of the "most favorable stipulations" to induce the proper man to devote himself to the task. "Favorable stipulations" he defined as the union, in one person, of the "position of a general and president of the council of war with the title of generalissimo, field marshal, etc."[17] No civil powers were demanded "with, perhaps, the single exception of the political negotiations with foreign powers."[18] The elasticity injected by the terms "etc." and "perhaps" is rendered more significant by rereading one of the opening sentences of the letter, "A military and political leader is wanted,"[19] noting the coördination of "political" with "military" as it stands there. In the formal presentation of the plan Kalb expressly left it to Franklin and Deane "to extend" as well as to change or carry out his propositions.[20]

A further point, one connected with republican security, is of peculiar interest to the present study. Broglie, it appears, very much feared that the Americans might suspect that monarchical ambitions lurked behind his plan. Thus it was that he in-

[14]Stillé, *op. cit.*, 393. See also above, p. 27.

[15]Kapp, *op, cit.*, 95.

[16]*Ibid.*, 95. Broglie asserted that even "in a good European army everything depends upon the selection of a good commander-in-chief; how much more in a cause where everything has yet to be selected and adjusted." *Ibid.*, 96-97.

[17]*Ibid.*, 96.

[18]*Ibid.*, 95.

[19]*Ibid.*, 95.

[20]*Deane Papers*, I, 431.

structed his agent to be "particularly explicit" in "the assurance of the man's return to France at the end of three years" since this assurance would "remove every apprehension in regard to the powers to be conferred, and . . . even the semblance of an ambitious design to become the sovereign of the new republic."[21] Again, he warned Kalb to "content" himself "with stipulating for a military authority for the person in question."[22] Finally he directed that these powers "should be limited in no respect, except in so far as to remove all danger of a too extensive use of the civil authority, or of ambitious schemes for dominion over the republic."[23]

Kalb, in his formal statement of the project suggested, intentionally or otherwise, the expansion of which the plan was capable. For one thing he drew a clear-cut comparison between the situation of the United States and that of the Netherlands "when they were yet groaning under the . . . tyranny of their sovereigns." On this basis he suggested "that the same conduct which was so advantageous to the republican establishment of the Low Countries would produce the same effect in the present case."[24] He emphasized the strength of the personal following which his candidate would be able to command.[25] Moreover, he bore witness to the ambitious character of Broglie, as, for example, by his suggestion that the generalissimo's return to Europe be ensured "in a more precise manner" by a treaty clause securing Broglie's "elevation . . . to the dignity of Duke and Peer of France."[26]

Kalb's connection with the plan is the more significant because of his mission to America at an earlier date. In reality an agent for the French minister Choiseul and sent out to investigate reports that a revolt was brewing in the English colonies[27] he had posed as "a German travelling for his pleasure."[28] His command of the English language and his ability to adapt himself to any

[21]Kapp, *op. cit.*, 96.
[22]*Ibid.*, 96.
[23]*Ibid.*, 97.
[24]*Deane Papers*, I, 427.
[25]*Ibid.*, 429.
[26]*Ibid.*, 429–431.
[27]Kapp, *op. cit.*, 46-51, 68-69.
[28]Quoted from letter of Colonel N. Rogers, Jan. 24, 1810, *ibid.*, 315. (Rogers assigned too early a date to the visit.)

society had probably enabled him to collect evidence "everywhere, from the drawing-room down to the grog-shop."[29] An American friend[30] testified that Kalb had often told him of the observations made during this trip. According to this testimony Kalb had been struck by "the universal prepossession" in favor of England, and "the almost instinctive hostility" to France. On the basis of these observations he had later asserted that nothing but the "highly injudicious and short-sighted conduct of the British ministry" could have caused the colonists to revolt.[31] Kalb's official reports, made within the year, were somewhat similar.[32] They did, however, include a prophecy that American independence would eventually be declared,[33] though they predicted a peaceful conclusion to the controversy then raging.[34] They positively denied that, in case of a resort to force, the colonists would be willing to accept French aid.[35] It will be recalled that in 1768, the year of Kalb's visit, the Americans were still professing loyalty to the British King and reverence for British institutions, and casting the blame for existing conflicts upon the British ministry.[36]

In the face of such observations how could Kalb support the project of Count de Broglie? Perhaps he did not realize the extent of its possibilities. Perhaps he believed the plan impracticable, even in its most limited application, but was unwilling to oppose his friend and patron.[37] Yet it is conceivable that he considered the plan practicable and advantageous to all concerned. As for the old antipathy to the French it would seem to be supplanted by petitions for French aid.[38] The American Declaration of Independence had forborne to attack monarchical institutions, despite its denunciation of the ruling King. Thus a European

[29]Kapp, *op. cit.*, 315.

[30]Colonel Rogers. He had been aide to Kalb at Valley Forge and elsewhere. *Ibid.*, 315, n.

[31]*Ibid.*, 315-316.

[32]*Ibid.*, 286-295.

[33]*Ibid.*, 287.

[34]*Ibid.*, 288.

[35]*Ibid.*, 288.

[36]Above, p. 13.

[37]On the relations of Kalb with Broglie see, for example, Kapp, *op. cit.* 86-87.

[38]Such as those being made by Silas Deane.

might easily fail to realize the reaction against centralized power which had followed the Declaration.[39]

Let us now turn to the fate of Broglie's plan in American hands. The available papers of Silas Deane contain no positive indication of his own opinion on the matter.[40] Contemporary characterizations of Deane were so influenced by the factional quarrels in which he was involved that it is difficult to estimate his probable attitude.[41] If Deane was really vain, ambitious, and easily dazzled by the brilliancy of the French capital,[42] he may have been a convert to the cause of Broglie. The thought that the plan was, perchance, secretly favored by the French Court may have led Deane to believe it could be put into effect. Kalb's support of the plan, in view of his personal observations in America, may have given it weight with Deane. The tendency to think the American cause hopeless, later evidenced by his support of English conciliatory proposals,[43] may have led him at this time to believe the American cause could not succeed unless it made use of French aid of the type suggested.

A more probable explanation is suggested by a report from Deane to John Jay respecting some supplies he was forwarding. He advised that they be examined for impositions, since he himself had been unable to examine them, they being guaranteed by "persons in such station" that a show of suspicion might have ruined his affairs.[44] He wrote in the same letter that he hoped the officers sent would "be agreeable," adding that they "were recommended by the Ministry" and were "really in their army," though this "must be a secret."[45] Franklin later wrote a defence of Deane which, though referring specifically to the affair of some French officers, may have had the Broglie plan also in mind.

[39]This reaction was to be seen in the state constitutions and the organization of the Continental Congress. Thomas Pownall's suggestion of a British stadtholder for the colonies (as part of his plan for imperial reorganization) is very interesting in this connection. See Pownall, *Administration of the British Colonies*, II, 84-86. He believed this idea incorporated in the Albany plan of union.

[40]On the fate of two lost volumes, see *Deane Papers*, I, intro., p. vii, and Jefferson, *Writings* (Washington ed.), II, 454–455.

[41]C. F. Adams, *Life of John Adams*, 280. (Vol. I of J. Adams, *Life and Works*.)

[42]*Ibid.*, 249.

[43]*Deane Papers*, I, pp. xii-xiii.

[44]Dec. 3, 1776, *ibid.*, I, 395.

[45]*Ibid.*, 397.

Its main point was that only a person on the spot could "know the infinite Difficulty of resisting the powerful Solicitations here of great Men, who if disobligd might have it in their Power to obstruct the Supplies he [Deane] was then obtaining."[46]

Apparently no direct evidence remains of the reception of the plan in America.[47] The recall of Deane in 1777 and the rejection of most of the officers sent by him[48] throw some light on the situation. The orders[49] for Deane's return were noncommittal as to the reason, but an undated motion based the recall on Deane's indiscretion in engaging French officers.[50] If Congress could not comply with such engagements "without deranging the Army, and thereby injuring, at this critical Juncture, the American Cause,"[51] how much less would Congress have accepted the Broglie plan!

Little evidence appears as to the reaction of the general public to the plan. Deane's proposition of December 6, 1776 was printed in a Pennsylvania newspaper, February 16, 1779.[52] This was done through the bad faith of Thomas Paine who had access to the letter when secretary to the Committee for Foreign Affairs.[53] The very manner of its publication probably lessened its effect. Samuel Adams said, speaking of another episode in Paine's attack

[46]Franklin, *Writings* (Smyth ed.), VII, 77. It will be recalled that Franklin and Arthur Lee were made joint commissioners with Deane late in 1776. Up to that time Deane was our sole representative in France. See C. Isham, "A Short Account of the Life and Times of Silas Deane," *American Historical Association Papers*, III, 41-43.

[47]See Wharton, *Diplomatic Correspondence*, I, 396.

[48]Kapp, *op. cit.*, 306.

[49]Resolution of Nov. 21, 1777, *Journals of the Continental Congress*, IX, 946-947. Order of Dec. 8, 1777, *ibid.*, 1008-1009. The activity of Deane's friends in Congress was said to account for the character of the recall. See S. Adams, *Writings*, IV, 71.

[50]Quoted in *Journals*, VIII, 605, n. 2. This probably was made on or about Aug. 5, 1777. Compare S. Adams, *Writings*, IV, 14.

[51]*Journals*, VIII, 605, n. 2. A very practical reason for this attitude was found in the threatened resignations of such officers as Generals Greene and Knox in case they were superseded by French officers. *Journals*, VIII, 537; Washington, *Writings* (Ford ed.), V, 404-406, n. Compare S. Adams, *Writings*, IV, 14.

[52]*Deane Papers*, III, 361-362. (The paper mentioned was the *Pennsylvania Packet*.)

[53]This committee was successor to the Committee of Secret Correspondence. See *Journals of the Continental Congress*, VII, 274.

on Deane, that its nature was such that Paine's "prudence . . . and even his Veracity was called in Question . . . and his Authority & Influence as a Writer of facts lessend."[54] Very likely the letter in question was suppressed as much as possible through a fear that its exploitation might anger the French court.[55]

John Adams in 1778 recalled having heard of the French project in Congress the preceding year. Curiously enough he connected it with Marshal Maillebois.[56] Having heard that this gentleman and Marshal Broglie[57] were reputed to be "the two most intriguing men in France," he wrote, "I was the more disposed to believe it of the former, because I knew of his intrigue with Mr. Deane to be placed over the head of General Washington in the command in chief of our American army."[58] A chance remark by Vergennes was noted by Adams as confirmation "of the design at court, of getting the whole command of America into their own hands, and a luminous commentary on Mr. Deane's letters, which I had seen and heard read in Congress, and on his mad contract with M. du Coudray and his hundred officers."[59] Adams recorded his own attitude as follows: "My feelings, on this occasion, were kept to myself, but my reflection was, 'I will be buried in the ocean, or in any other manner sacrificed, before

[54]S. Adams, *Writings*, IV, 134. Contrast the statement by Charles Lee, *Lee Papers*, III (*New York Historical Society Collections*, VI), 344, n. Lee stated that Deane had been accused of having "made some overtures to Prince Ferdinand of Brunswick, to accept the command of the American army," the very idea of which appeared "so very ridiculous" to "the foreign officers . . . acquainted with the prince's reputation as a soldier" that a mention of it threw them "into violent fits of laughter."

[55]S. Adams, who probably saw the letter of Dec. 6, 1776 (see *Journals of the Continental Congress*, VIII, 596), wrote that sitting "by a fire Side" with a friend he might tell things about Deane which he dared not write. S. Adams, *Writings*, IV, 111.

[56]M. Dubois (Broglie's secretary) hinted at the existence of competition for the position Broglie desired. Letter to Kalb, Dec. 17, 1776, Kapp, *op. cit.*, 92.

[57]The Marshal (or Duke) de Broglie does not appear to have had any share in his brother's project. It is worthy of note that Kalb gave Adams a letter of introduction to *Count* de Broglie when Adams was about to depart for France in 1777. J. Adams, *Works*, VII, 9.

[58]*Ibid.*, III, 146.

[59]*Ibid.*, III, 146. See also Stillé, *op. cit.*, 376-377, n. 1.

I will voluntarily put on the chains of France, when I am struggling to throw off those of Great Britain."[60]

This probably expressed the sentiments of all, or practically all, of the Americans who heard of the Broglie plan. While they professed to feel much gratitude to the French King[61] it did not extend, in general, to French officers. So far as any resultant exaltation of kingship was concerned this admiration for the French King was counterbalanced by the growing conviction that the British King, and not the ministry, was responsible for the war.[62] Doubtless the American poet, Freneau, writing in 1778, was warmly seconded when he said that nothing good could be said in behalf of kings in general, despite occasional good kings, and that,

"Though one was wise, and one Goliath slew,
Kings are the choicest curse that man e'er knew."[63]

If Count de Broglie[64] continued to cherish the project he must have been disillusioned, late in 1778, by the following letter from his chief agent in the affair:

"They [the Americans] are insultingly vain towards any nation but their own. . . . they have established their sovereignty alone without help (whereas they owe it to France) against the bravest and most powerful of nations; their General Washington is the first of all heroes ancient and modern; Alexander, Condé, Broglie, Ferdinand and the King of Prussia are not to be compared to him. . . . It is not only the lower classes;—clever people, or those passing for such, have the same opinion, and this is said so often, that Washington believes it himself."[65]

In the summer of 1780 an offer of negotiations looking towards

[60] J. Adams, *Works*, III, 146-147.

[61] See *Journals of the Continental Congress*, XII, 1139; J. Bowdoin to Franklin, May 1, 1780, *Massachusetts Historical Society Proceedings*, 2d ser., VIII, 285, 290; and President of Congress to Franklin, Oct., 1781, *Papers of the Continental Congress*, vol. 16, *President's Letter Book*, 1781-1787, Manuscripts Division, Library of Congress.

[62] J. Armstrong to W. Armstrong, Feb. 26, 178-, *William Armstrong Papers* (Force Transcripts), Manuscripts Division, Library of Congress; Franklin to D. Hartley, Feb. 3, 1779, Franklin, *Writings* (Smyth ed.), VII, 226, 227.

[63] Quoted in Tyler, *Literary History of the American Revolution*, II, 253.

[64] He did continue to plot against the British. See above, footnote 4, chapter II.

[65] Kalb to Broglie, Nov. 7, 1778, Stevens, *Facsimiles*, no. 1987.

reunion with the mother country was made to the Vermonters.[66] The offer appeared at an opportune time since the Green Mountain state was in a critical situation in 1780, and, indeed, during the following year. Thwarted in attempts to gain admittance to the Confederation,[67] threatened with a renewal of hostilities by her rivals New York, New Hampshire, and Massachusetts,[68] and peculiarly open to military invasion from Canada,[69] the state stood in need of some new expedient.

The offer was accepted by a small group of leading Vermonters, such as Governor Chittenden and Ethan and Ira Allen,[70] and the resulting negotiations were terminated only by the end of the war.[71] As carried on by the Vermonters their main characteristics may be listed as follows: First, a prolongation of the affair by repeated delays and postponements;[72] second, as a chief excuse for such a prolongation, the plea that only a cautious and gradual preparation would bring the mass of the people to the point of accepting the plan;[73] third, protestations of sincerity to the British on the one hand,[74] and on the other insinuations to the Americans that the real object was to deceive the enemy and to promote the

[66] *Vermont Historical Society Collections*, II, 59-61. General Haldimand, Governor of Canada, was the chief British intermediary. The sources for a study of this episode are found in the "Haldimand Papers" and supplementary data printed in the *Vermont Historical Society Collections*, II, 59-366. Some of the more important secondary accounts are in the volume just cited, pages 367-391, and in Ira Allen, *History of Vermont* (as reprinted in *Vermont Historical Society Collections*, I), 414-468; B.H. Hall, *History of Eastern Vermont*, 380-381, 412-414, 503, 721-724; J.L.Heaton, *The Story of Vermont*, 81-85, 87; S. Williams, *History of Vermont*, II, 201-218.

[67] *Vermont Historical Society Collections*, I, 373, 381, 401, 409, 452, 464; II, 24, 200; Williams, *op. cit.*, II, 217–218.

[68] *Vermont Historical Society Collections*, II, 30, 61, 86; also I, 330, 399-400, 419–420.

[69] *Ibid.*, II, 61, 86; and I, 419-420.

[70] Principally Colonel Ira Allen, Governor Chittenden, Major Fay, General Ethan Allen, and a few others, possibly including the majority of the governor's council. See *ibid.*, I, 428; II, 128, 159, 367. See also *Report on Canadian Archives, 1889*, 58.

[71] General Haldimand's last letter on the subject of Vermont was dated March 25, 1783. *Vermont Historical Society Collections*, II, 335.

[72] For examples see *ibid.*, II, 109-116, 122-123, 128, 143, 159, 191, and especially 335.

[73] *Ibid.*, II, 109-110, 112, 114, 122, 128, 143, 159, 172.

[74] *Ibid.*, II, 113, 128, 129, 158. The British apparently doubted this sincerity at times. See *ibid.*, II, 145, 148-149, 152, 158, 162, 179, 265, 273.

common cause by halting incursions from the north; [75] fourth, as the fundamental justification of their activities the assertion that the well-being of Vermont as a free and independent state, unhampered by New York or any other usurping rival, was a more cherished object with Vermonters than even the success of the revolutionary cause, in case the latter should not assure the former.[76]

The popular interpretation of these dealings has represented them as legitimate strategic deceptions of war, cleverly employed against the British.[77] But the lack, at the time, of a long-standing ideal of national existence, and the lack of cordiality towards Vermont on the part of the other states and Congress[78] give some basis for a different conclusion. While there is no reason to believe that the negotiators preferred Vermont's union with Great Britain, even as a separate province, to admittance, as a "free and independent state," to the Confederation[79] it is quite possible that some of the leading citizens of Vermont contemplated a return to the old allegiance as a last resort. In that event they expected support, not only from the Tories of the state but also among some of the rebels who had no preference for the "tyranny" of

[75] *Vermont Historical Society Collections*, II, 131, 135, 203. Compare 255. Vermont profited, during the remainder of the war, by what amounted to an immunity from attack by the British who wished to do nothing that would endanger the final success of the negotiations. Williams, *History of Vermont*, II, 215-216.

[76] *Vermont Historical Society Collections*, II, 109, 110-111, 117, 123, 128, 143, 191, 200, especially 117 and 123 and 158. Compare *ibid.*, 57, n. 1, 151, 200, 202, 265. B. H. Hall, in his *History of Eastern Vermont*, 413-414, presents some interesting anecdotes bearing on this point.

[77] Such treatment may be found in any of the accounts cited above, p. 36, n. 66, with the possible exception of Ira Allen's *History of Vermont*.

[78] Governor Chittenden besought military coöperation from various other states on the score that one of the alternatives for the Vermonters was to "*be under the disagreeable necessity of making the best terms with the British that may be in their power*" as any state might do "separately considered from their union." *Vermont Historical Society Collections*, II, 6, 34.

[79] They undoubtedly hoped that the realization that Vermont might renew her old allegiance to Great Britain would induce Congress to treat the state with more consideration than formerly. *Ibid.*, II, 9, 23-34, 148, 158; and I, 429. Compare and contrast Ethan Allen's assertions to Lord Dorchester in 1788, *Report on Canadian Archives, 1890*, State Papers, Calendar, 211.

Congress over the tyranny of Parliament and the King.[80] The situation of a royal province, with "every prerogative and immunity which is promised to other provinces," provided for a measure of local autonomy[81] which might appear attractive to Vermont, more eligible alternatives failing.

On the other hand, too much emphasis can hardly be put upon the conclusion that the mass of the people of Vermont were undoubtedly opposed to reunion with Great Britain. Their own actions, the statements of Allen and the other negotiators, and the final opinion of Lord Haldimand all confirm this view.[82] The latter's comment to Sir Henry Clinton, in October, 1781, is to the point. After stating that his "suspicions of Allen's party" are "almost, if not entirely, removed" he continued as follows: ". . . I see, with much concern, that the wished for revolution very little depends upon their[83] interest, at least as things are at present circumstanced. The prejudice of a great majority of the populace, and the prevailing influence of Congress, are too powerful to admit of a chance, (within any given time from one to three years,) by negotiation."[84]

Most significant to the present study is the fact that the negotiators made no special point of the superiority of republican to monarchical government. Instead they weighed their practical difficulties with Great Britain against those with their neighbors and the Confederation, without throwing theoretical advantages or disadvantages into the scale on either side.[85]

[80]Compare *Vermont Historical Society Collections*, II, 110, 117, 123, 158; I, 417. B. H. Hall states that the anger of the Vermonters against Congress rose so high after the congressional resolutions of December 5th, 1782, that many of a group at Westminster "damned the Congress, and for the toast drank their confusion, and the health of King George the Third of England." Hall, *History of Eastern Vermont*, 478.

[81]The French consul Crèvecoeur in a letter from Boston, July 27, 1787, expressed his belief that "les Vermontois n'y attachent plus la même importance" as formerly to a recognition by Congress of their independence. Letter to the Duke of Harcourt, C. Hippeau, *Le Gouvernement de Normandie*, III, 141-142. Ira Allen, in the negotiations in question, urged neutrality as the best stand for Vermont for the duration of the war. *Vermont Historical Society Collections*, II, 110.

[82]For a variety of evidence on this point see *ibid.*, I, 437, 460; II, 7, 77-80, 130, and especially 150, 179; also Williams, *History of Vermont*, II, 214-215.

[83]The reference is to the men of "Allen's party."

[84]*Vermont Historical Society Collections*, II, 179.

[85]Apparently and perhaps actually they upheld the dictum expressed in a couplet

The American victory at Yorktown and especially the return of peace which it forecast, operated powerfully to check whatever monarchical tendencies may have existed in Vermont.[86] Freed from the fear of military aggression, without the heavy burden of war debt under which her neighbors groaned, Vermont entered upon a period of peace and prosperity which, for a time, lessened her desire for admission to equal coöperation with the thirteen confederated states.[87] But the cessation of serious military activities brought to a head difficulties in another quarter, namely, the military encampment at Newburgh. The tendency to exalt General Washington, noticeable during the latter years of the War,[88] was about to reach an astounding climax in propositions to erect an American monarchy with Washington at its head. These propositions will be discussed in the following chapter.

by Pope which Ethan Allen is said to have had on the tip of his tongue [though he thundered it forth in quite a different connection than the case above noted]:

"For forms of government, let fools contest,
What e'er is best administer'd, is best."

B. H. Hall tells this anecdote in his *History of Eastern Vermont*, 342-343.

References were made, on the Vermont side, to the "Whig" principles of many of the Vermonters as a reason for delay in the negotiations (see for example *Vermont Historical Society Collections*, I, 435), but these principles were not made a point of defense or argument, unless the passages in the same volume, pages 117 and 123, be considered such, and these are not necessarily antimonarchical.

[86]*Ibid.*, II, 191, 251, 335; *Report on Canadian Archives, 1889*, 53, 58.

Nevertheless, even after news of peace had been received, the governor and council of Vermont apparently sought the advice of the Canadian governor as to the best course for Vermont to follow. See Ira Allen's account, *Vermont Historical Society Collections*, I, 467-468. An attempt to revive the reunion movement was made during the last months of Vermont's campaign to become the "fourteenth state." See below, pages 110-114.

[87]For assertions as late as 1794 that Vermont would not stand with the rest of the United States in case of war against England but would "support a neutrality" or "make the best bargain they can for themselves" see respectively "Governor Simcoe to Mr. Dundas" (*Report on Canadian Archives, 1889*, 57), and "Statement by Mr. Jarvis" (*ibid.*, 58). These assertions were based on remarks of "very respectable people of Vermont."

[88]Illustrated by the letter from Kalb to Broglie, above, page 35, and by the following:

Massachusetts Historical Society Proceedings, VII, 167; *New Jersey Archives*, 2d series, II, 135-137; "Belknap Papers," I (*Massachusetts Historical Society Collections*, 5th ser., II), 91, 300; Humphreys, *Life of David Humphreys*, I, 242; Charles Lee, *Papers*, III, 322, 372, 400-401; *Massachusetts Historical Society Collections*, 4th ser., X, 804.

CHAPTER III

MONARCHICAL TENDENCIES AT THE CLOSE OF THE REVOLUTIONARY WAR: THE PLAN OF COLONEL NICOLA

Probably the most dangerous problem during the months of uncertainty immediately following the Yorktown campaign was the unpaid and discontented army which had won the war. It has been said that "in the spring of 1782, the army would have made Washington king."[1] Lack of complete evidence may forever make impossible a final test of the truth of such a statement, but some definite conclusions may be drawn from the material available. Jefferson, ever alert to detect "monarchical" tendencies, believed that there had been "a cabal of the officers of the army who proposed to establish a monarchy and to propose it to General Washington."[2] Again he wrote: "Some officers of the army, as it has always been said and believed . . . trained to monarchy by military habits, are understood to have proposed to Genl. Washington . . . to assume himself the crown, on the assurance of their support."[3] He declared that "Steuben and Knox have ever been named as the leading agents"[4] and further implicated "Rufus King and some few civil characters" in the plot.[5] Washington "frowned indignantly at the proposition, [according to the information which got abroad,] . . . . " The supporters of the intrigue "never dared openly to avow it," knowing that popular opinion would oppose it.[6] Probably Jefferson had in mind rumors which had developed about the Newburgh Address and its attendant circumstances. But the most

[1]C. L. Becker, *Beginnings of the American People* (*The Riverside History of the United States*, I), 273. Compare J. Fiske, *Critical Period of American History*, 107; R. Hildreth, *History of the United States*, II, 421-422; and J. Sparks, *Writings of Washington*, VIII, 300-301, 301–302, n.; also W. C. Ford's edition of Washington's *Writings*, X, 22-24, n.

[2]Notes on Marshall's *Life of Washington*, Jefferson, *Writings* (Ford ed.), IX, 262, n. 1.

[3]Preface to "The Anas," Jefferson, *ibid.*, I, 157.

[4]*Ibid.*, I, 157.

[5]*Ibid.*, IX, 262, n. 1.

[6]*Ibid.*

definite and unequivocal monarchical propositions that have ever come to light are those made by Colonel Lewis Nicola in his letter to Washington May 22, 1782.[7]

Colonel Nicola was an Irishman by birth. Some time after rising to the rank of major in the British army he came to Philadelphia. This was about 1766, a period when a newcomer would probably have been impressed by the idea that the King—and kingship—were cherished by the Americans. He became an officer in the revolutionary army and was respected for his activities, especially as an organizer.[8] He had occasion, several times, to address General Washington in behalf of himself or as spokesman for other officers.[9] The courteous attention he received encouraged him [10] to approach Washington on the subject of an American monarchy. He explained that he had previously kept his ideas on the subject "within [his] own breast" because "Republican bigots [would] certainly consider [his] opinions as heterodox, and the maintainer thereof as meriting fire & faggots." He was confiding them now to Washington only in the strictest confidence and with the expectation of possible disapproval on the part of the latter, for, as he put it, "By freely communicating them to your Excellency I am persuaded I run no risk, & that, tho disapproved of, I need not apprehend their ever being disclosed to my prejudice."[11] On the other hand, in begging Washington to suspend judgment till he should have gone through "the whole, & not to judge of it by parts,"[12] Nicola certainly acknowledged a hope that Washington's final judgment might favor his propositions.

In explaining why he was broaching the matter at that particular time Nicola wrote:

"Possibly the event I forsee, may not, if at all, take place for a considerable time, but as that is uncertain, the purpose of the

[7]This is the date assigned by the authorities of the Library of Congress, Manuscripts Division.

[8]Born in Dublin, 1717, died c. 1807; *New International Encyclopaedia*, XVII, 134-135.

[9]See *Washington Papers, Correspondence with the Officers, Index*, 2713-2714.

[10]As he states at the opening of his letter containing the propositions. *Washington Papers*, vol. 198.

[11]"Nicola Propositions," p. 7, *ibid.*

[12]Nicola to Washington, May 22, 1782, *ibid.*

enclosed of moment, & must require mature deliberation, I choose not to defer mentioning it any longer."[13]

The army had been patient and long suffering, according to Nicola, for it had realized that the "particular circumstances of the times" had occasioned many of the injuries they had suffered. But "as the prospect of publick affairs cleared up, the means of fulfilling engagements encreased, yet the injuries, instead of being lessened, [had] kept pace with them." Nicola at no time questioned the good faith of Congress, but he apprehended that their good intentions could not be carried out because of "schemes of economy in the legislatures of some States, & publick ministers, founded on unjust & iniquitous principles." Under such circumstances there was a "dismal prospect" that when the army's services were no longer needed the army would be neglected and its members in many cases be reduced to beggary.[14] Nicola offered some interesting evidence to show that he was by no means alone in his forebodings, writing, "From several conversations I have had with officers, & some I have overheard among soldiers, I believe it is generally intended not to seperate after the peace 'till all grievances are redressed, engagements & promises fulfilled. . ."[15]

When one attempts to picture the actual carrying out of such intentions the bloody scenes of a civil war appear in the foreground. Nicola, however, expressly disclaimed such an outcome. "God forbid we should ever think of involving that country we have . . . rescued . . . into a new scene of blood & confusion," he exclaimed. Yet the members of the army were equally determined to claim their just rewards in order to provide for the subsistence of themselves and their families. The implied solution was to let them try their hand at constitution making, their brethren in civil life having failed so miserably in their attempts.[16] Such action seemed doubly reasonable to Nicola. In the first place, the members of the army had not been consulted "personally or representatively" in the framing of the governments under

[13]Nicola to Washington, May 22, 1782, *Washington Papers*, vol. 198

[14]"Nicola Propositions," p. 1, *ibid.* Also *ibid.*, p. 2.

[15]*Ibid.*, p. 2.

[16]*Ibid.*, p. 2.

which they were living.[17] In the second place, Nicola thought that the plan he had prepared had sufficiently provided for the general welfare[18] to be generally accepted, without any armed conflict.

Four features of his plan are of especial importance. First, his well argued defense of the superiority of monarchical features in governments and particularly in the "mixed government" of Great Britain; second, the connection with the plan of a military colony "to the west;" third, the attention to detail evidenced in much of the plan; fourth, the offering of the position of king to General Washington.

In defense of monarchy Nicola wrote as follows:

"I own I am not that violent admirer of a republican form of government that numbers in this country are; this is not owing to caprice, but reason & experience. Let us consider the fate of all the modern republicks of any note, without running into antiquity, which I think would also serve to establish my system."[19]

As may be expected the "republicks" which he considered were "Venice, Genoa, & Holland." These had, he said, "shone with great brightness, but their lustre [had] been of short duration, and as it were only a blaze." The reduced political importance of the Netherlands in particular concerned him, because of the "great similarity" between their form of government and that of the United States. In contrast, as he noted, the "principal monarchies of Europe" despite many difficulties, still shone with brilliancy. Even absolute monarchy was "more beneficial to the existence of a nation" than the republican form.[20] But better than this was the mixed form of government which had been most nearly perfected in England, as a result of "repeated struggles between prince & people."[21] Even this was "still short of perfection," but—and this is very important—the defects were of a nature to be easily excluded from the constitution of an American

[17]They had, instead, been "engaged in preventing the enemy from disturbing those bodies which were entrusted with that business." "Nicola Propositions," p. 2.

[18]*Ibid.*, p. 7.

[19]*Ibid.*, p. 2.

[20]*Ibid.*, p. 3.

[21]*Ibid.*, p. 4.

"mixed government." The remedies were to confine representation to counties and a "few large trading cities," giving the franchise to "all contributing to the support of government," and to make elections annual; also to secure the dependence of the king by allowing him "no command of money beyond what is requisite to the support of his family & court, suitable to the dignity of his station." Thus improved, "the constitution would approach much nearer to that degree of perfection to which sublunary things are limited." Another essential feature to the best "mixed government" was probably "some degree of nobility" but this, he conceived, might be "limited . . . not hereditary."[22]

Nicola then proceeded to the more concrete part of his suggestions. He pointed out that Congress as well as some of the states had already "promised all those that continue in the service certain tracts of land, agreeable to their grades. . . " To insure justice, said Nicola, "they ought all to be put on a footing" by the United States, with no discriminations between men from different states nor between those in the army at the close of the war and those earlier dismissed" through schemes of economy.[23] He continued:

"These things premised, I think Congress should take on itself the discharging all such engagements . . . by procuring a sufficient tract in some of the best of those fruitful & extensive countries to the west of our frontiers, so that each individual should have his due, all unprofitable mountains & swamps, also lakes & rivers . . . not to be reckoned as any part of the lots, but thrown in [for] the benefit of the whole community. *This tract to be formed into a distinct State under such mode of government as those military who choose to remove to it may agree on.*"[24]

The attention to detail, already noted, is most prominent in the next few paragraphs which deal with remedies for the depreciation of notes, the liquidation of public debts by instalments, one "to be paid immediately, to enable the settlers to buy tools for trades & husbandry, & some stock," provisioning the emigrants

[22]"Nicola Propositions," p. 4. (Note the similarity between these points and later reform platforms in England. Note also that the provision for annual elections might well be expected by Nicola to win favor for his plan from persons who might otherwise oppose it as too undemocratic.)

[23]*Ibid.*, p. 4.

[24]*Ibid.*, p. 5. (The italics are not in the original.)

at continental expense till sometime after the harvesting of the first crop, and so on.[25] This feature of the plan is of importance because it indicates that Nicola had given the subject much attention and quite probably had been present at group discussions of similar schemes.

It was at this point that Nicola at last ventured to make his most startling suggestion, which was as follows:

"This war must have shewn to all, but to military men in particular the weakness of republics, & the exertions the army has been able to make by being under a proper head, therefore I little doubt, when the benefits of a mixed government are pointed out & duly considered, but such will be readily adopted; in this case it will, I believe, be uncontroverted that the same abilities which have lead us, through difficulties apparently unsurmountable by human power, to victory & glory, those qualities that have merited & obtained the universal esteem & veneration of an army, would be most likely to conduct & direct us in the smoother paths of peace."[26]

Waxing bold with enthusiasm Nicola declared, "Some people have so connected the ideas of tyranny & monarchy as to find it very difficult to seperate them, it may therefore be requisite to give the head of such a constitution . . . some title apparently more moderate, but if all other things were once adjusted I believe strong arguments might be produced for admitting the title of king, which I conceive would be attended with some material advantages."[27]

In closing he returned once more to the idea of a western colony citing its services as a reason for the adoption of his plan by the country. He wrote:

"I have hinted I believed the United States would be benefited by my scheme, this I conceive would be done, by having a savage & cruel enemy seperated from their borders, by a body of veterans, that would be as an advanced guard, securing the main body from danger. There is no doubt but Canada will some time or other be a seperate State, and from the genious & habits of the people,

[25]"Nicola Propositions," pp. 5-6. The cost of the provisions mentioned was to "be deducted from each non commissioned & private mans debt" with the exception of provisions needed during the interval before the "accounts [were] all adjusted & the troopsr eady to march."

[26]*Ibid.*, pp. 6-7.

[27]*Ibid.*, p. 7.

that its government will be monarchical. May not casualties produce enmity between this new State & our Union, & may not its force under the direction of an active prince prove too powerful for the efforts of republicks? It may be answered that in a few years we shall acquire such vigour as to baffle all inimical attempts. I grant that our numbers & riches will encrease, but will our governments have energy enough to draw them forth? Will those States remote from the danger be zealously anxious to assist those most exposed? Individuals in Holland abound in wealth, yet the government is poor & weak."[28]

Washington's stern rebuke to Nicola is far better known than is Nicola's presentation of his case.[29] One may well agree with Professor Channing that "Washington's reply is, possibly, the grandest single thing in his whole career."[30] It deserves praise, not only for its spirit of renunciation, but also for its recognition that the American people had become fundamentally anti-monarchical in sentiment. Yet someone should speak in behalf of Nicola. He too, despite his errors of judgment and his personal—even selfish—interest, wished well to America.[31] Probably the country, more than once, has been rescued from disaster by the tremendous powers of its chief executive, especially in time of war. There have been occasions when Nicola, could he be imagined as an interested though invisible spectator, might have reflected that some of the features of his plan had actually been put into force.

Attention should be called to another letter to Washington written but a month after the Nicola propositions. It vividly

[28]"Nicola Proposition," p. 7.

[29]Washington to Nicola, May 22, 1782, *Washington Papers*, vol. 198, Manuscripts Division, Library of Congress. Washington, *Writings* (Sparks ed.), VIII, 300-301; *ibid.* (Ford ed.), X, 21-22. A brief summary of Nicola's propositions and two quoted paragraphs are given by Sparks in a footnote, VIII, 301-302. Sparks believed Nicola was voicing the sentiments of a party in the army, "neither small in number, nor insignificant in character . . . ." Ford follows Sparks. See Washington's *Writings* (Ford ed.), X, 22-24 n. Nicola's secret was faithfully kept. Other men were, by rumor, connected with a monarchical plot of 1782 but not Nicola. See, for example, the *Aurora*, Aug. 30, 1800, p. 2, where Hamilton is accused in a letter dated April 25, 1795.

[30]Channing, *History of the United States*, III, 376.

[31]The three letters of apology which he wrote to Washington help one to understand Nicola and his motives. As they appear not to have been printed elsewhere they are given in full in an appendix to the present study. See below, pages 129-134.

expressed a feeling of despair over the existing situation, and suggested an "absolute Monarchy, or a military State," as the only salvation "from all the Horrors of Subjugation."[32] Its writer, like Nicola, was interested in a colony, to the west, as shown by his later prominent connection with the Ohio Company.[33] The letter was written by Major General James Mitchell Varnum under the heading "Providence, June 23d 1782." Varnum was, at the time, an officer in the Rhode Island militia and a member of Congress,[34] having previously resigned his commission as Brigadier General in the Continental army.

After referring to certain other subjects he burst forth with this exclamation:[35]

"Such is the dreadful Situation of this Country that it is in the Power of any State to frustrate the Intention of all the others—This Calamity is so [manuscript torn at this point] Founded in the Articles of Confederation, and will continually increase 'till that baseless Fabric shall yield to some kind of Government, the Principles of which may be correspondent to the Tone of the Passions. The Citizens at large are totally destitute of that Love of Equality which is absolutely requisite to support a democratic Republick: Avarice, Jealousy & Luxury controul their Feelings, & consequently, absolute Monarchy, or a military State, can alone rescue them from all the Horrors of Subjugation.—The circulating Cash of the Country is too trifling to raise a Revenue by Taxation for supporting the War,—& too many of the People are obstinately averse to those artificial Aids which would supply its Deficiency. In this Situation every Moment augments our Danger, by fixing the Habits of Licentiousness, and giving Permanency to British Persevearence: And should Dejection in our Ally proceed to Misfortune,[36] the Instability of national Policy may give Place to the Sentiments of the mediating Powers, 'that we are too young to

[32]General J. M. Varnum to General Washington, June 23, 1782, *Washington Papers*, vol. 198, Manuscripts Division, Library of Congress.

[33]See, for example, A. B. Hulbert, *Pilots of the Republic*, 119, and S. P. Hildreth, *Pioneer History*, 246-247.

[34]*Appletons' Cyclopaedia of American Biography*, VI-VII, 261. On the ability and standing of Varnum as a lawyer see A. C. McLaughlin, *The Confederation and the Constitution* (*The American Nation*: *A History*, X), 152.

[35]Varnum to Washington, June 23, 1782, *Washington Papers*, vol. 198.

[36]This refers, no doubt, to the naval victory of Rodney over de Grasse, the middle

govern ourselves.'—At all Events, this Country hangs upon the Issue of the present Campaign! If a great Exertion could be made, . . . to repossess ourselves of New York, we may possibly realize the Blessings of Independence; But Time alone will unfold the Decrees of Fate."

General Washington's answer to Varnum was very different from the one he had written to Nicola.[37] He observed that Varnum's state had met its obligations better at least than the other states. He added that "tho' the conduct of the people at large" was "truly alarming" he could not "consent to view" the situation "in that distrest light" in which Varnum saw it. He concluded with the hope that even yet "some fortunate Crisis will arrive, when those destructive passions, which I confess too generally pervade all Ranks, shall give place to that love of Freedom which first animated us in this Contest."

Six years later General Varnum delivered the first Independence Day oration at Marietta, Ohio.[38] Part of his remarks on that occasion were so pertinent to the subject of the letter just considered that they should be considered at this point. He said in part:

". . . the articles of the confederation, founded upon the union of the states, were so totally defective in the executive powers of government, that a change in the fundamental principles became absolutely necessary, and but for those friendships which have formed and preserved an union sacred to honor, patriotism, and virtue, and, but for that superior wisdom which formed the new plan of a federal government, now rapid in its progress to adoption, the confederation itself, before this day, would have

of April, 1782. (On this victory see Van Tyne, *The American Revolution*, 328.) Compare letter by Washington to R. R. Livingston, May 22, 1782, *Washington Papers*, 198.

[37]Under date of July 10, 1782, *Washington Papers*, vol. 198. Perhaps Washington made some allowance for what appears to have been the rather excitable temper of the man. See G. Morris on Varnum, Washington, *Writings* (Ford ed.), VII, 30, n. 1. An odd characterization by T. Rodney (in Congress with Varnum , April 13, 1781, is as follows: "A resolution was moved by Genl. Varnum . . by words like the Man himself . . . . fine . . . but not well adapted to the occasion." T. Rodney, *Diary*, 38-39, Manuscripts Division, Library of Congress. Washington's previous correspondence with Varnum shows that they had been mutually concerned over the mutinous spirit in the army. Washington, *Writings* (Ford ed.), VII, 328, n.

[38]Hildreth, *Pioneer History* 504.

been dissolved! Then, indeed, might we have 'hung our harps upon the willows, for we could not have sung in a strange land.' Then we might have lamented, but could not have avoided the horrors of a civil war. Promiscuous carnage would have deluged the country in blood, until some daring chief, more fortunate than his adversary, would have riveted the chains of perpetual bondage!

"But now anticipating the approaching greatness of this country, nourished and protected under the auspices of a nation, forming and to be cemented by the strongest and the best of ties; the active, the generous, the brave, the oppressed defenders of their country will here find a safe, an honorable asylum, and may recline upon the pleasure of their own reflections."[39]

It is customary to make some allowance for the patriotic fervor of the moment when quoting a speech of this nature. Such caution may well be discarded in this case when it is compared with the yet more impassioned outburst of the confidential letter of 1782.[40] The second paragraph suggests a reason for the non-fruition of monarchical projects, namely, that a solution was found which was much better suited to the republican and democratic tendencies of the people at large.

The dissolution of the confederation hinted at by Varnum had been, about 1782, a common subject of discussion, if we may trust the notes of a foreign observer. Even members of Congress often discussed them, and professed to feel little fear for disastrous results of such a course.[41] Another view of the subject regarded the confederation as a convenient interstate treasurer, but little more.[42] Meanwhile the financial distress of the army did not become less acute. A more distinguished officer than either Nicola or Varnum, and later first governor of the Northwest Territory, wrote thus in November, 1782:

[39]Hildreth, *op. cit.*, 506.

[40]Reference has already been made (above, n. 37) to the excitable temper of Varnum. While this might argue that he might exaggerate difficulties it equally argues that he, though little more alarmed than his friends, would be a better informant because less cautious in his expression of his thoughts.

[41]Translator's comment, *Travels by Marquis de Chastellux*, I, 218-219. The sojourn in Philadelphia during which the translator heard these discussions was probably early in 1782. See *Massachusetts Historical Society Proceedings*, XI, 6.

[42]See, for example, R. H. Lee, *Letters* (J. C. Ballagh ed.), II, 282.

"I am in debt, and my credit exhausted, and, were it not for the rations I receive, my family would actually starve."[43]

Washington himself, a few weeks earlier, had written to the Secretary of War, "I can not help fearing the result of the measure in contemplation, [the reduction of the army] . . . when I see such a number of men, goaded by a thousand stings of reflection on the past and of anticipation on the future, about to be turned into the world, soured by penury and what they call the ingratitude of the public. . . ." What the result was which Washington so feared is shown by the last sentence of the paragraph, "On the other hand, could the officers be placed in as good a situation as when they came into service, the contention, I am persuaded, would be, not who should continue in the field, but who should retire to private life."[44]

The "Newburgh Addresses" and the "Order of the Cincinnati" are familiar terms to any one who has read the history of this period. Both had become factors in the American situation early in 1783. Their connection with "monarchical tendencies" is a matter of conjecture and interpretation, yet deserves some notice.

The "Addresses"[45] and the circumstances surrounding them lend themselves to our purposes as a commentary on the Nicola propositions. It will be recalled that the first of these papers was a petition to Congress, "agreed to by the principal officers" of the Newburgh cantonment. The petition contained nothing startling.[46] James Madison noted that General McDougall (member of the committee which presented the address to Congress) "made a remark w.ch may deserve the greater attention as he stepped from the tenor of his discourse to introduce it, and delivered it with peculiar emphasis. He said that the most intelligent & considerate part of the army were deeply affected at the debility and defects in the federal Gov.t, and the unwillingness of the States to cement & invigorate it; as in case of its dissolution, the benefits expected from the Revolution w.d be greatly impaired, and as in particular, the contests which might ensue am.g the States would be sure to embroil the officers . . . "[47] Thus it seems evident

[43]Gen. St. Clair to Gen. Washington, Nov. 26, 1782, *St. Clair Papers* (W. H. Smith ed.), I, 572.

[44]Oct. 2, 1782, Washington, *Writings* (Ford ed.), X, 92.

[45]Conveniently treated in J. Sparks, *Writings of Washington*, VIII, appendix XII

[46]*Ibid.*, 551-552.

[47]*Madison's Notes on Debates in the Continental Congress*, Jan. 13, 1783.

that there was a general feeling among the officers that the existing government was very faulty and that there was little chance of its reform through civil action.

It will be recalled that the second "Newburgh Address" was unofficial and anonymous.[48] It is probable, however, that these very characteristics, since they meant a certain freedom from restraint, more truly expressed the existing discontent. Nicola had merely reported hearing that the army intended to refuse to disband till the pay they felt due them should be assured beyond doubt.[49] The author of the second "Newburgh Address" boldly urged such action by the army.[50] Another feature of this address reminds one of Nicola's plan, for there was a suggestion that, under certain circumstances, the officers, "courting the auspices, and inviting the direction" of their "illustrious leader" should "retire to some unsettled country." The author showed scorn for neither monarchy or republicanism as such but rather for the oppression that might be manifest under either. Thus he exhorted his fellow officers to oppose tyranny when it was garbed in the "plain coat of republicanism" quite as much as when it assumed the "splendid robe of royalty."[51]

It has been said that probably "Hamilton himself, and others generally patriotic, were not altogether sorry to see the army restless."[52] Such an attitude could be easily accounted for by a desire for justice to public debtors and sure tranquility for the country[53] without connecting it with monarchical tendencies. A record of the confidential talks in which Hamilton probably took part, along with men of similar views, such as Gouverneur Morris for example, would throw much light on our problem. But no record of the sort appears. General Washington coped with the Newburgh affair quite as successfully as he had rebuked the monarchical propositions of Nicola. The meeting of officers which he addressed on the subject thanked him for what he had said, and

[48]Evidence points to "John Armstrong, aide-de-camp to General Gates" as the writer, and to Gates, alone or with other "conspicuous men", as the instigator. McLaughlin, *The Confederation and the Constitution*, 65.

[49]"Nicola Propositions," p. 2.

[50]J. Sparks, *Writings of Washington*, VIII, 557.

[51]*Ibid.*, 557.

[52]McLaughlin, *op. cit.*, 60.

[53]Compare *ibid.*, 62-63.

"resolved unanimously, That the officers of the American army" rejected "with disdain, the infamous propositions"[54] of the anonymous address. They even made the following resolve:

"That the army continue to have an unshaken confidence in the justice of Congress and their country; and are fully convinced, that the representatives of America will not disband or disperse the army until their accounts are liquidated, the balances accurately ascertained, and adequate funds established for payment."[55]

The military officers were not much longer without an organization which would continue to exist even after the disbanding of the army. In fact they looked forward to future generations and made their organization hereditary. It has a place in the present study despite the fact that the founders of the Society of the Cincinnati[56] had no "monarchical" intentions judging by their papers and private correspondence. Even Aedanus Burke, who combatted them with his anonymous pamphlet, which appeared soon after the society was founded,[57] admitted this, though he believed that they might have cherished such ideas in their hearts.[58] That is mere conjecture. But there are two points in connection with the Cincinnati which should be brought to mind in a study of monarchical tendencies, first, the popular hostility to the society, and second, its potentialities as a political machine. Neither of these had become very apparent in the first few months after the close of the war.[59] The further consideration of them will therefore be deferred to later chapters.

[54]J. Sparks, *Writings of Washington*, VIII, 560-565.

[55]*Ibid.*, 564.

[56]Founded May 13, 1783, at General Steuben's headquarters near Fishkill, N. Y. Its purpose, as stated, was to continue comradely intercourse among the officers and provide for needy members. Provision was made for 13 state societies, to send delegates triennially to a general convention. Washington was its first president, succeeded after his death by Hamilton. It barely continued throughout the 19th century but is now in existence again with its full number of branches. *New International Encyclopaedia*, V, 335-336.

[57]*Considerations on the Cincinnati.* Burke was a judge in South Carolina, and famous for his distaste of ceremony. See *American Historical Association Report, 1896*, I,885-887. Although as a member of the convention in his state he opposed the adoption of the new federal constitution he served in Congress 1789-1791. *Appletons' Cyclopaedia of American Biography*, I, 454.

[58]Burke, *op. cit.*, 3.

[59]*Ibid.*, 3.

A few days after the organization of the Cincinnati Society a mutiny of some troops at the seat of the confederated government evidenced in a menacing fashion the resentment of the army over the matter of unfulfilled congressional promises.[60] Among the members of Congress forced to flee before the insulting demonstrations of the mutineers were probably men destined later to become so disgusted with the weakness of the existing government as to manifest decidedly monarchical inclinations.[61]

The remainder of the year was comparatively uneventful. The official news of the signing of the definitive treaty of peace at last arrived in October. Already, in anticipation of this news, the army had been reduced, and on November third all remaining members who had enlisted for the duration of the war, were discharged.[62] General Washington, after some final arrangements, departed for his plantation and private life.[63] If the American people was thinking of monarchical rank for him it appeared to be only after he should die, when he might sit upon one of the

> ". . . thrones erected in the taste of heav'n,
> Distinguish'd thrones for patriot demi-gods".[64]

[60] A most interesting contemporary account of this is found in *Madison's Notes on the Debates in the Continental Congress*, June 19-21, 1783.

[61] For instance Nathaniel Gorham. See below, 69.

[62] F. L. Humphreys, *Life of David Humphreys*, I, 279.

[63] "Washington arrived at Mount Vernon on the day before Christmas." Washinton, *Writings* (Ford ed.), X, 340, n. 1.

[64] From an ode "To His Excellency General WASHINGTON," by "Hortensius" (Governor William Livingston), written for the *New-Jersey Gazette* in the spring of 1778, *New Jersey Archives*, 2d ser., II, 135-137.

CHAPTER IV

MONARCHICAL TENDENCIES FROM THE END OF THE WAR TO THE CONSTITUTIONAL CONVENTION: THE PRINCE HENRY EPISODE

By the time Congress had ratified the peace treaty (in January, 1784) the army had been quietly dispersed. But the fact that Congress "could barely assemble a quorum to ratify the treaty"[1] is illustrative of the more or less demoralized state of the government and suggests further trouble ahead. It is quite possible that that there has been a tendency to paint the "Critical Period" in too somber colors. Many people of the time seem to have been fairly comfortable and contented under their state governments despite the defects of Congress.[2] The Articles of Confederation had been received with signs of "joy . . . in every Countenance but those of the Disaffected."[3] As late as January 1786 a prominent New England business man praised the government of the Confederation for its "many excellent principles" and explained its apparent defects as "impediments in its administration" rather than in its structure.[4]

[1]Jan. 14th. Van Tyne, *The American Revolution*, 330.

[2]See for example *The Letters of R. H. Lee*, II, 284, 343.

[3]Thomas Rodney, *Diary*, Feb. 26, 1781; Manuscripts Division, Library of Congress. Rodney was a member of Congress from Delaware at the time of the final adoption of the Articles of Confederation. By "the Disaffected" Rodney seems to have meant a minority out of sympathy with the general trend of affairs in the new nation.

[4]Nathan Dane in letter of Jan. 20th, *Dane Letters*. Manuscripts Division, Library of Congress. His sincerity in moving for a constitutional convention was questioned by Madison in his *Notes on Debates in the Continental Congress*, Feb. 21, 1787. Manuscripts Division, Library of Congress. On Dane's public services see *Massachusetts Historical Society Proceedings*, II, 7-9. In a letter of Jan. 31, 1786, Dane said it was yet "too early to take desperate measures" but if "3 or 4 weak or obstinate States" would not contribute properly to the general funds they "must be shaken off and left to their misfortunes." *Dane Letters*, Jan. 31st. Compare J. B. McMaster, *History of the People of the United States*, I, 201-202.

On the other hand it will be recalled that the Congress of the Confederation had so little power that it could not even provide for the debts which had been part of the price of independence. The president of Congress in 1787 was almost in despair over the disgraceful difficulty of securing a quorum, while his predecessor has been suspected of seeking truly desperate remedies.[5] In general Congress failed to command respect either at home or abroad.[6] It was the unrest in New England particularly, culminating in the "Shays Rebellion," which is generally accepted as having convinced men, all over the United States, of the absolute necessity of a reform of the government of the Confederation. But comparatively little attention has been paid to the possibility that the more stringent remedies which some of the Massachusetts conservatives considered pointed towards monarchical institutions.

The historian Minot, clerk of the Massachusetts House of Representatives at the time of the insurrection, wrote that "There began . . . to arise [a] class of men in the community, who gave very serious apprehensions to the advocates for a republican form of government. These, though few in number, and but the seeds of a party, consisted of persons respectable for their literature and their wealth. They had seen so much confusion arising from popular councils, and had been so long expecting measures for vindicating the dignity of government, which seemed now less likely to take place than ever, that they, with an impatience too inconsiderately indulged, were almost ready to assent to a revolution, in hopes of erecting a political system, more braced than the present, and better calculated, in their opinions, to promote the peace and happiness of the citizens."[7] In the Massachusetts convention for the ratification of the federal constitution a Mr. Smith, who described himself as "a plain man" and farmer and no office seeker, declared that the insurrection of the preceding year had brought so much anarchy and distress that "we should have been glad to snatch at anything that looked like a govern-

[5] Arthur St. Clair to Governor Huntington of Connecticut [June or Aug.?] 1787; *St. Clair Papers*, I, 603-604. (The letter does not specify the month or day.)

[6] See such standard treatments as that by Fiske, *The Critical Period of American History*; McLaughlin, *The Confederation and Constitution*; McMaster, *op. cit.*, chaps. II-IV; Channing, *History of the United States*, III, chap. XV.

[7] G. R. Minot, *History of the Insurrections in Massachusetts* (1st ed., Boston, 1788, 2d ed., Boston, 1810), 61-62. For brief notice of Minot see *New International Encyclopaedia*, XV, 757.

ment. Had any person, that was able to protect us, come and set up his standard, we should all have flocked to it, even if it had been a monarch."[8] This statement, isolated though it be, at least suggests the possibility that the harassed people might have supported the projects of the little group of anti-republican leaders to whom Minot referred.

Jefferson, despite his own vigorous denunciations of monarchy as a remedy far worse than any disease that might afflict republican government,[9] could believe that some Americans were capable of considering monarchy for their country. "We were educated in royalism; no wonder if some of us retain that idolatry still."[10] Already, in 1784, a prominent New England clergyman had said, "Experiment is the surest and fairest way of coming at knowledge; and I think it will not be much longer before we shall all be convinced that a democratic government, over such a large and increasing number of people, inhabiting so vast an extent of country, is to say the least . . . extremely inconvenient . . . . and very inadequate to the purpose." Again he wrote, "Let it stand as a principle that government originates from the people; but let the people be taught (. . . they will learn it by experience, if no other way) that they are not able to govern themselves . . . .Should even a limited monarchy be erected, our liberties may be as safe as if every man had the keeping of them solely in his own power."[11]

William Plumer, in 1784, on the eve of his career as a prominent New England statesman, had no aversion to monarchy. Moreover he professed to believe his attitude to be a not unrepresentative one! His political creed was as follows:

[8]J. Elliot, *Debates in the . . . State Conventions*, II, 102-103.

[9]". . . with all the defects of our constitutions, whether general or particular, the comparison of our governments with those of Europe, are like a comparison of heaven & hell. England, like the earth, may be allowed to take the intermediate station." Jefferson to J. Jones, Aug. 14, 1787, *Writings* (Ford ed.), IV, 438. Compare his letter to B. Hawkins, Aug. 4, 1787, *ibid.*, IV, 426.

[10]To James Madison, Mar. 15, 1789, Jefferson, *ibid.*, V, 83. Note that in the same letter he is confident that the "young people . . . educated in republicanism" will never consider monarchy. Compare *ibid.*, IV, 261.

[11]Jeremy Belknap to Ebenezar Hazard, Feb. 27 and March 3, 1784, *Belknap Papers*, I (*Massachusetts Historical Society Collections*, 5th ser., II), 307 and 315 respectively. Belknap was prominent and respected in both Massachusetts and New Hampshire. See *New International Encyclopaedia*, III, 96.

". . . I am fully resolved to use my power & influence in supporting that form of Government which my country establishes. I do not feel hostile to either democracy, autocracy, or monarchy. I am inclined to think the people are much more interested in the good administration than in the theory or form of the government—Or, as Pope expresses it, 'That government is best which is administered best.' "[12]

John Jay, in 1786, after referring to the Shays Rebellion, wrote, "Much, I think is to be feared from the sentiments which such a state of things is calculated to infuse into the minds of the rational and well-intended. In their eyes, the charms of liberty will daily fade; and in seeking for peace and security, they will too naturally turn towards systems in direct opposition to those which oppress and disquiet them.

"If faction should long bear down law and government, tyranny may raise its head, or the more sober part of the people may even think of a king."[13]

Four months earlier Jay had written a similar letter to Washington[14] in which, without using the term "king" or "monarchy" he had confessed his fear that a "state of fluctuation and uncertainty must disgust and alarm" the "better kind of people"[15] until it should "prepare their minds for almost any change that may promise them quiet and security." Washington, in his answer, went much further and said he had been told "that even respectable characters speak of a monarchical form of government without horror." He added that "[f]rôm thinking proceeds speaking; thence to acting is often but a single step," and expressed horror at "consequences we have but too much reason to appre-

[12]*A collection of Letters written to and by William Plumer and transcribed for his Amusement and Instruction*, 58-59. Manuscripts Division, Library of Congress. See W. Plumer Jr., *Life of William Plumer*, 53-59. In a letter written the same year Plumer declared that "if our elective government" was to be "long supported" it would be due only to the judiciary, since this was "the only body of men" who had "an effective check upon a numerous Assembly." Plumer, *Letters*, 69. See *Life of Plumer*, 67-80.

[13]Jay to Jefferson, Oct. 27, 1786, Jay, *Correspondence*, III, 213.

[14]Written at Philadelphia, June 27, 1786. *Ibid.*, III, 203-205.

[15]Jay defined the "better kind of people" as those who were "orderly and industrious . . . content with their situations and not uneasy in their circumstances." *Ibid.*, 205.

hend."[16] Again, in December 1786, Washington was writing about the Massachusetts situation. This time it was in a letter to General Knox in which he noted that the latter had intimated "that the men of reflection, principle, and property in New England, feeling the inefficacy of their present government" were "contemplating a change" but that he had not been "explicit with respect to its nature."[17] Only a few weeks before the Constitutional Convention Washington expressed the following views in a letter to Madison: "I am fully of opinion that those, who lean to a monarchical government, have either not consulted the public mind, or that they live in a region, which (the levelling principles in which they were bred being entirely eradicated) is much more productive of monarchical ideas, than are to be found in the southern States. . . . I am also clear, that, even admitting the utility, nay, necessity of the form, yet that the period is not arrived for adopting the change without shaking the peace of this country to its foundation." This affords not only additional evidence that Washington recognized the existence of "monarchical" tendencies but suggests that he was not wholly horrified at their existence.[18]

Judging from the dearth of contemporary references to the "monarchical plot" of 1786 no one who knew the facts cared— or perhaps, dared— to be explicit about them, while the secret was too well guarded to be handed about among its enemies. It has been well and wisely said that "Imperfection or absence of record excuses many a lame and ill-constructed story and covers with a decent pall the failings of many a reputation."[19] Perhaps the story that a Prussian prince was offered an American crown falls under this indictment. But in view of the apprehensions of such men as Washington and Jay that something of the sort might be afoot the story should be examined, both by itself and in the light of attendant circumstances.

A newspaper article which appeared March 2, 1799, posed as having the facts well in hand. This article purported to be by a Federalist and, according to the editorial note, was printed in the

[16]Mount Vernon, Aug. 1, 1786, Washington, *Writings* (Ford ed.), XI, 55.

[17]Dec. 26, 1786, *ibid.*, XI, 105.

[18]Letter dated March 31, 1787, *ibid.*, XI, 132.

[19]W. C. Ford, Manuscripts and Historical Archives, *American Historical Association Report, 1913*, I, 79.

opposition press because it displayed "the sentiments and designs as well as the practices of the party that has been running these States to destruction . . ."[20] The letter impresses one as a clever parody of Federalist views. Whether a parody or not it is interesting and suggestive. The writer, after suggesting a royal dynasty for America, continued, "I have no idea however, of looking for one of a foreign growth. The invitation given to a Prince of the illustrious house of Brandenburgh, about the time of the Shays insurrection, never met my approbation: Henry's answer displayed great political sagacity, and ought never to be forgotten: I believe it still in existence." This disclosure was apparently not followed up. A monarchical charge in the same paper, more than a year later, contained no reference to the foreign prince, though it concerned "the period between the peace of 1783, and the formation of the constitution of 1787." It was aimed at Alexander Hamilton, as was also a similar rumor of about the same time which Hamilton flatly denied.[21]

Some fifteen years later President-elect Monroe confided to General Andrew Jackson his observations on monarchical tendencies in the period in question.[22] "That some of the leaders of the federal party entertained principles unfriendly to our system of government I have been thoroughly convinced; and that they meant to work a change in it, by taking advantage of favorable circumstances, I am equally satisfied." He then referred to his membership for three years in the Congress of the Confederation "just before . . . the adoption of the present Constitution," and later in the Senate, "beginning shortly after its adoption."

[20]The (Philadelphia) *Aurora* (reprinting from the *Albany Register*), Mar. 2, 1799, p. 2.

[21]*Ibid.*, Aug. 30, 1800, p. 2. For Hamilton's action concerning such charges see his letters to Governor George Clinton, Feb. 27, Mar. 2, Mar. 7, and Mar. 9, 1804, in Hamilton, *Works*, VIII, 610-613. James Kane records that he accompanied Hamilton in a call upon Mr. Purdy, who had repeated these charges, and Purdy said that what he had really said was in respect to a claim that "sometime previous to the convention which framed the present Constitution of the United States . . . somebody in England had made proposals to somebody at the Eastward for establishing a monarchy in this country, and placing at the head . . . a son of the King of Great Britain; that some letters or papers containing these proposals were sent to Gen. Hamilton, copies of which were made in his office to be distributed." *Ibid.*, VIII, 611, n. This version of Purdy's charges differs materially from that given by Mr. Kane.

[22]Dec. 14, 1816, Monroe, *Writings*, V, 342-345.

During this service, said he, "I saw indications of the kind suggested. It was an epoch at which the views of men were most likely to unfold themselves, as, if anything favorable to a higher toned government was to be obtained, that was the time. . . No daring attempt was ever made, because there was no opportunity for it." After making further comments apparently referring to the period following 1789, he concluded, "Many of the circumstances on which my opinion is founded took place in debate, and in society, and therefore find no place in any public document. I am satisfied however that sufficient proof exists, founded on facts, and opinions of distinguished individuals, which became public, to justify that which I had formed." He added that it was his "candid opinion . . . that the dangerous purposes . . . were never adopted, if they were known, especially in their full extent, by any large portion of the federal party; but were confined to certain leaders and they principally to the eastward." Even so he felt he ought to hesitate before admitting recruits from the Federalist party into his own administration. The practical politics of 1816 were interwoven by the writer with the monarchical charges which he made. Yet the existence of a political motive in circulating such charges does not prove that they were not founded on facts.

A more definite statement was made by President Monroe in 1817, according to the "Memoirs" of Joseph Gardner Swift.[23] The occasion was a confidential conversation which occurred sometime during a trip on which Swift accompanied the President. Swift records that "Mr. Monroe said that during the presidency of Congress of N. Gorham, that gentleman wrote Prince Henry, of Prussia, his fears that America could not sustain her independence, and asked the prince if he could be induced to accept regal power on the failure of our free institutions. The prince replied that he regretted deeply the probability of failure, and that he would do no act to promote such failure, and was too old to commence new labors in life."[24]

[23] J. G. Swift, 1783-1865, was one of the first two graduates of West Point. He was superintendent of the same from1812-1817. His *Memoirs* were published in 1890. For brief notice see *Lamb's Biographical Dictionary*, VII, 269-270.

[24] J. G. Swift, *Memoirs*, 164. Dr. Samuel Eliot Morison called the writer's attention to this passage.

In 1824 a diary entry by Rufus King bore witness that Monroe was still referring to the existence of monarchical tendencies.[25]

"10th May 1824. Col. Miller this evening said to me, speaking of Mr. Pr. Monroe that he had told him that Mr. Gorham, formerly President of Congress, had written a letter to Prince Henry, brother of the great Frederic, desiring him to come to the United States to *be their King*, and that the Prince had declined by informing Mr. Gorham that the Americans had shown so much determination agt. their old King, that they wod. not readily submit to a new one; Mr. Monroe adding that Genl. Armstrong had given him this information and that the papers or correspondence was in the hands of *General Hull.*[26]

"This communication arose from the letter of Monroe to General Jackson, expressing his opinion that among the Federalists of the time of Genl. Washington, were persons in favor of Monarchy, ! ! ! "

No communication of this nature appears among the Monroe papers, yet it is not improbable that it was transmitted orally. The question naturally arises as to how Armstrong knew that Hull had such papers, supposing they really were in his possession. He may have become aware of them during the court-martial of Hull in 1813-1814[27] since he was Secretary of War at the time.[28] On the other hand the papers may have been destroyed by fire, in 1812, along with many others belonging to Hull.[29] But Arm-

[25]R. King, *Life and Correspondence*, VI, 643-644. It may be relevant to remark that this again was the year of a presidential election.

[26]Hull's oration before the Massachusetts Cincinnati July 4, 1788 contains references quite in keeping with a knowledge of such a plan as the one ascribed to Gorham. See below, page 73.

[27]F. S. Drake, *Memorials of the Cincinnati of Massachusetts*, 352.

[28]*New International Encyclopaedia*, II, 157.

[29]For remarks on the loss of these papers see Drake, *op. cit.*, 353, and Marie Campbell, *Life of Hull*, ix-x. The latter was one of General Hull's daughters. She makes no reference to monarchical ideas in American unless a passage on page 218 refers to them. In connection with Hull's possible interest in the affair, it may be noted that he returned to Massachusetts about 1786 and took part against the Shays Rebellion. Drake, *op. cit.*, 346. He had served in the Revolution under Steuben. Campbell, *op. cit.*, 127. Incidentally it may be borne in mind that the charges against Hull dealt with treachery as well as cowardice although he was not convicted of the former.

strong had an opportunity for more direct information for he spent the winter of 1787–88 in the same lodging-house as General Steuben,[30] the man who is supposed to have transmitted the invitation to the prince.[31] He was, moreover, esteemed and trusted as a friend by Steuben.[32] If, as seems probable, Armstrong wrote the second "Newburgh Address,"[33] he was keenly interested in methods of curbing republican "tyranny."

Already, in 1822, two years before his diary entry on the subject, King had become involved in a sharp argument in the Senate regarding "a proposal of inviting some German prince" to an "intended American throne."[34] In 1825 there seems to have been an attempt to exploit the incident, probably as propaganda against King, who was being considered for the appointment to the Court of St. James.[35] Senator Barbour of Virginia, who had been King's opponent in the Senate argument on the matter, was called to account by King's son, Charles, and asserted that what he had said on that occasion "was stated as a mere rumor" and without pointing "to any particular individual, for none by name had been mentioned to him, so far as he then recollected." According to Barbour, King had entered the fray of his own accord, becoming much excited and denouncing the rumor "as most idle and unfounded." After some attention to the matter in high quarters, including a cabinet meeting, President John Quincy Adams concluded that "henceforth Prince Henry of Prussia" would be "suffered to sleep in Peace."[36] But the royal ghost has once more been aroused by a recent documentary discovery.

Until this discovery General Steuben's reputed participation in the episode rested upon an anecdote related by Mr. Mulligan,

[30]F. Kapp, *Life of Steuben*, 543.

[31]Below, pp. 63-64.

[32]Kapp, *op. cit.*, 585.

[33]See McLaughlin, *The Confederation and the Constitution*, 63-65. See also above, page 51.

[34]In the debate on the revolutionary pension act of Feb. 4, 1822. See Barbour's account of it in King, *Correspondence*, VI, 645-646.

[35]See King *Correspondence*, VI, 582, 644-647, for letter, etc., on the affair. See also J. Q. Adams, *Memoirs*, VII, 55, 56, 63-64; VI, 481.

[36]There appears to be no real reason for connecting King with the episode. Instead he seemed to have feared that some of the Massachusetts delegates to the Federal Convention would be men who would propose some such desperate remedies. See King, *Correspondence*, I, 201.

his secretary, many years after Steuben's death. Steuben's biographer, Friedrick Kapp, who heard the tale from Mulligan, considered the latter a trustworthy source despite the lapse of years since his association with the General.[37] Kapp relates that when "before the adoption of the present Constitution, in a circle of his [Steuben's] friends, the question of the form of government was discussed, and it was not yet decided whether the President was to be vested only with the authority of the highest civil officer, or with the more princely privileges of the Dutch Stadtholder, one of the party, addressing himself to Steuben, asked whether Prince Henry, of Prussia, would be willing to accept an invitation, and whether he would make a good President? Steuben answered, 'As far as I know the prince he would never think of crossing the ocean to be your master. I wrote to him a good while ago what kind of fellows you are; he would not have the patience to stay three days among you'."[38] Steuben was on intimate terms with such men as Duer, Jay, Hamilton and others of their standing, some of whom may have been in the group at the time.[39]

There is every reason to presume that Steuben took part in the affair. In the first place Prince Henry had been both friend and commander to Steuben in the days before the latter had transferred his military activities to America.[40] Even if he believed that Henry would refuse the invitation he might well have been pleased to transmit such a compliment to the Prince. In the second place Steuben, despite his very valuable services in the Revolution, had been treated by Congress with ingratitude and even injustice.[41] In the third place, Steuben took a keen interest in both the theory and practise of government.[42] Finally, his success in reorganizing the American army at a critical period during the War[43] may have led him to believe he could be equally helpful in reorganizing the government of his adopted country in the critical period succeeding the War.

[37]Kapp, *Life of Steuben*, xii, 584.

[38]*Ibid.*, 584.

[39]*Ibid.*, 580-581.

[40]*Ibid.*, 60-61.

[41]*Ibid.*, ch. xxv.

[42]*Ibid.*, 584. He wrote several articles on the prerogatives and duties of the chief executive officer under the republican form of government and was one of the active Federalists in New York politics.

[43]*Ibid.*, 526.

Several years ago there was discovered, in the Royal Prussian Archives at Charlottenburg, a copy of a letter written by Prince Henry to General Steuben in April, 1787. This find appears to have shed new light on the alleged invitation to the Prussian prince. Richard Krauel has given it to us as follows:[44]

"Monsieur de Stuben, général au service des États-Unis de l'Amérique. En Amérique au Hanôvre à 5 milles de New-York.
Monsieur

Votre lettre du 2 du mois 9bre m'est parvenue. Je l'ai reçue avec tout le sentiment de la reconnaissance mêlée de surprise. Vos bonnes intentions sont bien dignes de mon estime, elles me paraissent l'effet d'un zèle que je voudrais reconnaître, tandis que ma surprise est une suite des nouvelles que j'apprends par la lettre d'un de vos amis. J'avoue que je ne saurais croire qu'on pût se résoudre à changer les principes du gouvernement qu'on a établi dans les États-Unis de l'Amérique, mais si la nation entière se trouverait d'accord pour en établir d'autres, et choisirait pour son modèle la constitution d'Angleterre, d'après mon jugement je dois avouer que c'est de toutes les constitutions celle qui me paraît la plus parfaite. On a l'avantage que si, comme dans tous les établissements humains, il se trouve quelquechose de défectueux, qu'on pourrait le corriger et faire de si bonnes lois pour que la balance fût mieux établie entre le souverain et les sujets, sans que ni l'un ni les autres ne pussent jamais empiéter sur les droits alloués respectivement à chacun. Il ne m'est pas possible de vous envoyer un chiffre, vous comprenez qu'il courrait les hasards des lettres et se trouverait entre les mains de ceux qui s'en saisiraient les premiers. Je vais cet automne en France, peut-être y trouverais-je un de vos amis. Les Français sont jusqu'à cette heure les vrais alliés des États-Unis de l'Amérique. Il me paraît que rien de grand pourra solidement se faire chez vous, à moins d'y faire concourir cet allié. Cela suffit, Monsieur, pour vous faire comprendre que c'est par ce canal que je pouvais recevoir à l'avenir les lettres que vous voudrez m'adresser.

En vous assurant que je désire ardemment de vous donner des preuves de l'estime avec laquelle je suis, Monsieur, votre très affectioné ami."

[44] In an article, "Prince Henry of Prussia and the Regency of the United States, 1786," *American Historical Review*, XVII, 47-48. For the assignment of date to the letter see *ibid.*, 48.

Krauel admits that the letter does not, at first sight, appear to be an answer to monarchical propositions. But he points out that the phraseology was intentionally general and indefinite to avoid detection by outsiders who might get possession of the letter. He notes that the answer shows that the missive from Steuben inclosed a paper from an American friend of Steuben's of a nature to astonish the Prince. He asserts that the enclosure obviously "related to a proposed fundamental change in the constitution of the United States." The praise bestowed by Henry upon the English constitution, according to Krauel's suggestion, indicates that the Prince had monarchy in mind as a model. Krauel lays much stress on the fact that a Prussian prince was being consulted in regard to the internal politics of the United States, and that the consultation was to be so confidential as to involve a request that the Prince send a cipher for its continuance. Krauel asserts that the inference is almost sure that Henry, in his letter, was actually referring to a monarchical project but suggesting a French prince for the rôle.[45] Krauel admits that "strict proof in the legal sense" is lacking but concludes, "That the American writer of the letter which so astonished the prince was Nathaniel Gorham and that Gorham acted in a common understanding with his political party associates can scarcely be doubted longer."[46]

The missing letter has not yet been found and perhaps never will be.[47] Unless it appears and is seen to be of the character ascribed to it by such an account as the one set forth above the episode to which it relates is no sure proof of the existence of monarchical tendencies in the United States, although it may serve as a tentative guide pointing towards some such conclusion. In the absence of the letter some insight may be gained by a study of the life and character of the American who is said to have written the

[45] Krauel, *op. cit.*, 48-49.

[46] *Ibid.*, 51. Channing believes that Krauel has succeeded in demonstrating 'the strong probability" that a "suggestion was made in 1786 by some one looking toward the offering of the regency of the new United States to Prince Henry of Prussia . . ." *History of the United States*, III, 475. Farrand says that Krauel "presents interesting evidence" on the subject. *Framing of the Constitution*, 174.

[47] The present writer has communicated with such authorities as Worthington C. Ford, Archer B. Hulbert, J. Franklin Jameson, and Samuel E. Morison, only to be told by each that he knows of the existence of no "Gorham Papers" that would bear upon this subject. Appeals to members of the Gorham family have brought similar replies.

invitation to the Prince. Nathaniel Gorham was a leading figure among those citizens referred to as the "better kind of people," the "orderly and industrious," the "respectable," "rational," and "well-intentioned" who were suspected, in 1786, of leaning towards monarchy as a remedy for "vindicating" the much abused "dignity of government." An account of his life and public services[48] impresses one with his zeal for "good government" and his high standing among his constituents. He was born in Charlestown, Massachusetts, in 1738, and received his education in that town. His interest in history and in the biographies of great men, first evidenced in his school days, was maintained throughout his entire life.[49] About the close of the French and Indian War he entered business as a merchant in his home town.[50] He soon became a representative to the colonial legislature of Massachusetts and after that a member of the provincial congress and of the board of war. He served in the state constitutional convention of 1779.[51] About this time he acted as one of three commissioners who were influential in suppressing an incipient insurrection in western Massachusetts.[52] He was an active member of the Continental Congress in the years 1782 and 1783.[53] Some obscurity surrounds his movements for the next year. He was not in Congress and he may have been in Europe. Dr. Welsh, in an oration a few days after Gorham's death, refers to Gorham as having been requested by the sufferers from the Charlestown fire "to undertake a voyage to Europe" to solicit aid for the rebuilding of the town. Dr. Welsh does not state quite clearly that the trip

[48]For brief notices see Farrand, *Records of the Federal Convention*, III, 87-88; *Biographical Congressional Directory*, 679; Lamb, *Biographical Dictionary*, III, 336; R. Hildreth, *History of the United States*, III, 460; *American Historical Association Report, 1896*, I, 704; *Massachusetts Historical Society Collections*, 7th ser., III, 85-86, *Massachusetts Historical Society Proceedings*, 1st ser., XIX, 406, n. For longer accounts see Dr. Thacher, *Sermon on the Death of N. Gorham*, and Dr. Welsh, *Eulogy to the Memory of N. Gorham.*

[49]Welsh, *op. cit.*, 5-6.

[50]*Ibid.*, 5-6.

[51]Lamb, *Biographical Dictionary*, III, 336. See *Massachusetts Historical Society Collections*, ser. 7, III, 85-86 for the appointment of Gorham as a member of a Massachusetts commission to meet commissions from other states to consider problems connected with the war, July, 1780.

[52]Welsh, *op. cit.*, 10-11.

[53]*Journals of the Continental Congress*, XXIII, 811. 821, etc.; Madison, *Notes*, Jan. 15, Jan. 27, Feb. 11, etc., 1783.

was actually made.[54] At any rate he again entered Congress in 1785 and June 6, 1786, was elected successor to John Hancock as president of that body, a position he filled until February 2, 1787.[55] He was one of the Massachusetts delegates to the Federal Convention which framed our present constitution. He shared with Washington the honor of presiding at its meetings, acting as chairman of the committee of the whole.[56] He was an active supporter of the proposed constitution in the Massachusetts ratifying convention.[57] About this time he became associated with the "Phelps and Gorham's Purchase" of lands in western New York[58], the project for which he is probably best remembered today. In 1791 he was made "supervisor of the excise in the Massachusetts district."[59] His chief public services in these last years appear to have been in the capacity of judge of the Court of Common Pleas, a position he resigned only a few days before his death in 1796.[60]

As to his character and reputation the few references that we find regarding them are entirely favorable. Dr. Thacher said that there were few men who had "filled so many and important offices . . . and . . . to such general acceptance" and referred to his "wisdom and integrity" as being well-known. Dr. Welsh enlarged upon the same topics when he declared that "Few men were more perfect in the art of rendering themselves agreeable to public bodies. His knowledge of men unfolded to him all the avenues to the heart." Praise was bestowed upon the clear mind and the prudent and conciliatory temper which Gorham possessed.[61] Madison's notes on debates in the Continental Congress pictured Gorham as somewhat more assertive and less conciliatory than does the above account. One of his colleagues in the Constitutional Convention of 1787 described him in the following terms:

[54]Welsh, *op. cit.*, 11.

[55]Lamb, *Biographical Dictionary*, III, 336; Hildreth, *History of the United States*, III, 460.

[56]Farrand, *Records of the Federal Convention* I, 29-312, *passim.*

[57]Below, page 70.

[58]*Massachusetts Historical Society Proceedings*, XIX, 406, n.

[59]*American Historical Association Report, 1896*, I, 783, n.

[60]Welsh, *op, cit.*, 11.

[61]Thacher, *op. cit.*, 21-22; Welsh, *op. cit.*, 12. Compare Farrand, *op. cit.*, III, 87.

"Mr. Gorham is a Merchant in Boston, high in reputation, and much in the esteem of his Country-men. He is a Man of very good sense, but not much improved in his education. He is eloquent and easy in public debate, but has nothing fashionable or elegant in his style;—all he aims at is to convince, and where he fails it never is from his auditory not understanding him, for no Man is more perspicuous and full. He has been President of Congress, and three years a Member of that Body. Mr. Gorham is about 46 years of age, rather lusty, and has an agreable and pleasing manner."[62]

A remarkable feature of the man is that he seems seldom to have committed his thoughts to writing. Not only does it seem impossible to locate any collections of "Gorham Papers" but other collections of the period contain very few letters from Gorham. Even his letter book of correspondence as president of Congress is not to be found. Perhaps the prudence cited by his eulogist led Gorham to put little into writing and to preserve still less of what was written. Perhaps his preoccupation with action made him a poor correspondent and chronicler. Whatever the explanation, the fact remains a serious obstacle to a complete understanding of the man.

Some idea of Gorham's political views can be gained from the many references to his part in congressional debates in 1783. Judging by these records he subordinated theory to practicability,[63] and believed in making a fair trial of one expedient before abandoning it for another.[64] He supported vigorous action by Congress,[65] but with the interests of his own state and section especially at heart. He went so far as to hint that the formation of a New England confederacy might become advisable.[66] In his service in Congress in 1782 and 1783 he had much provocation to

[62]William Pierce, of Georgia, whose character sketches of various members of the Convention are of considerable interest and value. See Farrand, *op. cit.*, III, 87.

[63]Madison, *Notes*, for Jan. 15 [14], and Feb. 12, 1783.

[64]*Ibid.*, Jan. 15 [14].

[65]*Ibid.*, Jan. 27, Feb. 11.

[66]*Ibid.*, Feb. 21.

be discouraged and disgusted with the inefficiency of the existing government.[67]

Gorham's position as presiding officer during most of his last term in the Congress of the Confederation has deprived us of the remarks he might otherwise have made in debates in the eventful year of 1786, the year in which his letter to Prince Henry is supposed to have been written. A few bits of data, however, are available. For instance we find that he was a member of a committee appointed March 19, 1786, to attempt to persuade New Jersey to rescind a negative on a requisition proposal, New Jersey's action having caused "great uneasiness" in Congress.[68] The matter was still troubling him after his election as President of Congress, judging from a letter addressed to him by Governor Bowdoin of Massachusetts, who wrote, "I am of opinion with you that unless the States are more attentive to the requisitions of Congress . . . the federal government must cease and the union with it." Bowdoin suggested that "such a catastrophe" might be prevented by an urgent application to Governor Clinton in regard to New York's action on the impost act.[69]

The next year, as before noted, Gorham was a prominent member of the Federal Convention. The records show no attempt on his part to promote such a plan as the one concerning Prince Henry. He was always found, however, on the side of those who favored comparatively "high toned" measures.[70] One remark he made may be of marked significance, namely, that "It is not to be supposed that the Govt will last long enough" to make the numbers of representatives excessive, for "Can it be supposed that this vast Country including the Western territory will 150 years hence remain one nation?"[71]

Soon after the close of the Federal Convention Gorham was applying his energies towards the ratification of the new constitu-

[67]Madison, *Notes*, Jan. 24, Feb. 18, Feb. 20. Note especially the insulting conduct of the mutineers towards members of Congress, June 13-June 21. Gorham was doubtless one of the fleeing Congressmen who adjourned to meet at Princeton. On conditions in Congress, 1786-1787, see King, *Correspondence*, VI, 199.

[68]Monroe, *Writings*, I, 124.

[69]Letter of June 24, 1786. *Bowdoin and Temple Papers*, II (*Massachusetts Historical Society Collections*, 7th ser., VI) 104.

[70]See Farrand, *op. cit.*, III, 660-661, for index references to Gorham's part in the Convention.

[71]Aug. 8, 1787, Farrand, *op. cit.*, II, 221.

tion by the Massachusetts state convention. He sought and secured from Franklin permission to publish the latter's closing speech made in the Federal Convention, declaring it a speech "calculated to prevent war and blood-shed."[72] In the Massachusetts convention he "vindicated the delegates to Philadelphia against the charge of exceeding their commission"[73] and "explained the nature of the President's office; the advantage of the responsibility of *one man*, &c."[74] Gorham expressed great joy at hearing of the ratification of the Constitution by Virginia. In a letter on the subject to Washington he wrote thus:

"Although I am passing rapidly into the vale of years, and shall live to see but a small portion of the happy effects which I am confident this system will produce for my country, yet the precious idea of its prosperity will not only be a consolation amid the increasing infirmities of nature and the growing love of retirement, but it will tend to soothe the mind in the inevitable hour of separation from terrestrial objects."[75]

There is a variety of evidence which supports the hypothesis that monarchical tendencies were developing in Massachusetts and perhaps other parts of the North towards the end of the Confederation period. In the summer of 1787 St. John de Crèvecoeur, French Consul at New York, was visiting friends in Boston.[76] Crèvecoeur had spent much of his life in America[77] and was much interested in strengthening the connections between France and the United States.[78] But July 22, 1787, he wrote,[79] "I wou'd not advise an European who is possessed of

[72]Thus he secured permission from Franklin to publish his closing speech in the Convention, and apparently found it effective propaganda. See Hays, *Calendar of Franklin Papers*, IV, 357, 361, and *Franklin Papers, Miscellaneous*, VIII, 1840.

[73]Jeremy Belknap's notes on the Massachusetts ratifying Convention, *Massachusetts Historical Society Proceedings*, III, 302.

[74]*Ibid.*, 301.

[75]July 21, 1788, G. Bancroft, *History of the Constitution of the United States*, II, 475.

[76]According to Julia P. Mitchell, *St. Jean De Crèvecoeur*, 266. Crèvecoeur spent "most of July, all of August, perhaps part of the autumn as well" in Boston.

[77]*Ibid.*, 11-13.

[78]He had been active in establishing a packet service between the two countries. *Ibid.*, 3.

[79]In a letter to William Short in Paris. The letter quoted is in the possession of the Historical Society of Pennsylvania. The present writer is indebted to Dr. John W. Jordan, Librarian, for permission to have a copy made for use in this study.

some property to visit this Country just now. . . ." The reason he advanced was that "it [is] made Extremely Precarious by the weakness of Gov^{t} and the horrid abuse the people have made ot their Legislatif Power." After exclaiming over the "astonishing change" that had taken place "in the Laws & Gov^{t} of ye Americans" he added, "Some time I cant help wishing the Independants had been postponed to a more distant period—if the Federal Convention is able to accomplish nothing all will be Lost for the Seeds of broils & Contentions are ready to burst in many Places." A possible and even probable source for some of his ideas is revealed in a matter of fact postscript, "I saw yesterday Col. Humphreys[80] at Govr Bodouin."[81] Knowing the aristocratic tendencies of these two men, and knowing that both had been following the Massachusetts uprising with keen interest and much foreboding[82] it is wholly reasonable to conclude that they felt as pessimistic as did Crèvecoeur. His half wish for a return of monarchy may well have been an echo of wishes he heard expressed in Governor Bowdoin's presence.

As late as April 1, 1788, the same writer made some yet more startling statements.[83] One can read them today in the original, though only with great difficulty, since the letter in which they occur is written in an almost illegible hand.[84] The passage of greatest interest, when translated into English, reads as follows:

"Would You believe, that in the 4 Provinces of New England they Are So weary ["las"] of the Govt. . . . that they Sigh for Monarchy & that a very large number of persons in several Counties would like to return to English domination (?)—Lord Dorchester Govr of Canada has Spies on All Sides, This City

[80]For Humphreys' aristocratic manner see F. Humphreys, *Life of David Humphreys*, III, 387, 429.

[81]On Bowdoin see *Massachusetts Historical Society Proceedings*, 2d ser., XI, 291; *Proceedings of American Antiquarian Society*, n. s., XV, 223.

[82]Above, p. 69, and Humphreys, *op. cit.*, I ,373-374, 378. Two letters from Crèvecoeur to the Duke of Harcourt written at about the same period describe the political situation with much more reserve. C. Hippeau, *Le Gouvernement de Normandie*, III, 136-152.

[83]Letter to William Short, New York, April 1, 1788, *Short Papers*. Manuscripts Division, Library of Congress.

[84]The poor penmanship is not characteristic of the other Crèvecoeur letters in the Library of Congress. Miss Emily Mitchell, of the Manuscripts Division, kindly assisted in the reading of this letter.

[New York] is full of them.[85] . . .[86] This Country Approaches an Epoch more . . . dangerous than that of the War. . . . I hope that this Store ["Masse"] of . . . good Sense for which this country is so distinguished, . . . will . . . make the balance Lean to the right Side; it remains to be Known, how men who have been without restraint and law for so long a Time will Submit Themselves to the salutary restraint which is prepared for them."

The interest in an English ruler, here indicated, became most evident during the sitting of the Convention of 1787 as will be noted in the following chapter. The passage has been quoted at this point, however, because of its description of the state of mind that seems to have suggested the Prince Henry plan.

On December twenty-seventh, 1787, Nathan Dane remarked of the proposed constitution, "I doubt whether it has monarchy enough in it for some of our Massachusetts men, nor democracy enough for others."[87] A few days later General Knox, to whom this letter had been addressed, wrote to Washington that perhaps many of the party "for the most vigorous government" [a party including about "three-sevenths" of the State] "would have been more pleased with the new constitution had it been still more analogous to the British Constitution."[88] This use of the term "monarchy" might, however, refer to such features, say, as a long term for senators or great powers for the president.[89] For this reason an apparently less equivocal statement is of special interest. Such a statement was made by Benjamin Tupper[90] in April, 1787. Addressing Knox he wrote:

[85]Compare letter of Nov. 9, 1787, to Jefferson in which Crèvecoeur says he will even fight for the new constitution, despite his age, and if it fails he will try to leave the country for it "will become the scene of anarchy and confusion." Mitchell, *op. cit.*, 338.

[86]In the passage omitted there seems to be an assertion that the whole country will fall, once a part has broken itself off.

[87]To General Knox, *Essex Institute Historical Collections*, XXXV, 89.

[88]Jan. 14, 1788, Drake, *Life ansd Correpondence of Henry Knox*, 97.

[89]The matter of definition has not become an essential part of this study up to this point. It will be considered in succeeding chapters.

[90]On Tupper see *Appletons' Cyclopaedia of American Biography*, VI-VII, 180; Drake, *The Cincinnati of Massachusetts*, 489-490; McMaster, *History of the United States*, I, 505-507, 323.

"Perhaps your Honor may remember that on my return from the Ohio I declared in favour of Majesty for which your Honor gave me a gentle check . . . I cannot give up the Idea that Monarchy in our present situation is become absolutely necessary to save the States from sinking into the lowest abbiss of Misery. I have delivered my sentiments in all companies at this term, without reserve, and was, and am exceedingly pleased to find such a respectable number of my sentiments. I am clearly of Opinion if matters were properly arranged it would be easily and soon effected. The Old society of Cincinnati must once more consult and effect the Salvation of a distracted Country. While I remain in the Country [until removing to Ohio] I shall be a strong advocate for what I have suggested . . ."[91]

Colonel Tupper was not alone in his theory that the "Order of the Cincinnati" might prove itself an instrument for some such plan. This was the very charge brought against it by its opponents.[92] But when one seeks to find expressions of the idea by the members of the society he is baffled. Written proof shows only that the Cincinnati kept up their esprit de corps and their support of orderly government.[93] General Hull, who delivered the Independence Day address to the Massachusetts Cincinnati in 1788, rejoiced in the "happy prospect of bidding . . . farewell to a feeble system, which could neither shield you from external invasion, or protect you from internal commotion. . ." Incidentally, before discussing the promise of relief in the new constitution, he took occasion to eulogize America's ally, King Lois XVI, concluding, "Illustrious Monarch, but more illustrious by your virtues than your crown, long may you live the patron of the rights of man— . . . and may your reign be ever glorious." He congratulated his hearers on the fact that peaceable remedies were being applied in the United States instead of "the mad career of the ancients" which overwhelmed "the most celebrated

[91]Quoted by A. E. Morse, *Federalist Party in Massachusetts*, 42, n. 5.

[92]For examples see Burke, "*Considerations on the Cincinnati*," especially pp. 3, 4, 6-8, 11; *Belknap Papers*, I, (*Massachusetts Historical Society Collections*, 5th ser., II) 277, 303, 307; S. Adams, *Works*, IV, 298-299; Drake, *The Cincinnati of Massachusetts*, 29, 34; Drake, *Life of Knox*, 146, 148; and *Massachusetts Historical Society Proceedings*, 2d ser., VIII, 178. For an amusing satirical attack see Franklin, *Works* (Smyth ed.), IX, 161-168.

[93]This was evidenced in their services against the Shays Rebellion. See especially Knox to Washington, Jan. 14, 1787, Drake, *Life of Knox*, 148.

republicks." Indirectly he praised the Cincinnati for having "chearfully relinquished their arms, when [their country's] safety was obtained" at the end of the War.[94] But there is a significant identity of leadership in a number of groups of the time, namely, the New England Cincinnati, the Newburgh Petitioners, and the members of the Ohio Company.[95] The absence of written evidence does not prove that others than Varnum and Tupper did not share their views.[96] Professor Hulbert, an undoubted authority on the correspondence of the promoters of the Ohio Company and allied enterprises, has said that "these men were close-mouthed business men; their objects and methods are rarely, if ever, stated in writing; adept in the art of communicating unessentials," they were "past masters in the art of refraining from writing at all."[97] A letter of the type of the Tupper letter, then, was an unusual burst of confidence. General Tupper did not hear the Independence Day oration in which Varnum announced his faith that the new Constitution, once adopted and in operation, would cure the ills of the time,[98] but he probably would have subscribed to these sentiments.

If anybody is to be convicted of promoting a monarchical plan for any or all of the United States it must be on circumstantial evidence. Unless different data appear such conclusions as the following are probably the only justifiable ones: First, that letters of the period bear out later charges, and that some persons in the United States, at least up to 1788, actually favored a monarchical government; second, that there is a reasonable probability that Gorham and some other leading citizens were ready to support such a change; third, that although there was a report that the Governor of Canada was following developments with suspicious care, the evidence, for the most part, points to the consideration of a Prussian, rather than an English prince;[99] fourth,

[94]Hull, *Oration . . . to the Cincinnati*, 14, 11, 20.

[95]A. B. Hulbert, *Records of the Ohio Company*, I, xl-xli, gives some suggestive statistics on this identity of leadership. Gorham does not appear to have taken part in these enterprises but must have been in touch with some of the participants through his activities in business and politics.

[96]Above, p. 47.

[97]Hulbert, *op. cit.*, I, lxxiv.

[98]Tupper did not arrive at Marietta till the month after this oration was delivered. See Drake, *The Cincinnati in Massachusetts*, 490.

[99]More attention will be paid to this point in the following chapter.

that as the tendency appeared to be almost entirely confined to New England, and this, too, at a time when the idea of the Union was too little advanced to be elevated to the end in itself that it later became, the plan may have been for a New England monarchy, including in time New York;[100] fifth, that the known character and public record of the men involved proves the motives to have been a desire for general security of property and "good government;" last, that the extreme caution which marked the utterances of the men probably most interested indicates that something of a "coup d'état" was the only method thought feasible for the change, and this indicates that it was expected that the people would, in general, oppose the change at first, but that their aversion would in time be overcome by the benefits to be received in peace, order, and prosperity.[101]

[100]Dr. Samuel Eliot Morison, in a letter to the present writer, has said of the later secession movement in New England, "In all the correspondence regarding New England Separatism I have never seen any suggestion that the Northern Confederacy should be anything but a republic." Speaking of the Federalists in general, before 1788, he says that "there was a tendency" on their part "to grasp at the monarchical idea, as a drowning man grasps at a straw." See also H. Adams, *Documents relating to New England Federalism.*

[101]See above, page 56.

CHAPTER V

MONARCHICAL TENDENCIES IN THE UNITED STATES DURING THE FRAMING OF THE PRESENT CONSTITUTION

The need of constitutional reform was sufficiently agreed upon in Congress by February 21, 1787, to produce a resolution that a convention be held "for the sole . . . purpose of revising the Articles of Confederation" and for reporting to Congress and the state legislatures such provisions as they should agree necessary to "render the federal constitution adequate to the exigencies of Government & the preservation of the Union."[1] The twelve states that appointed delegates[2] were, in general, slow in getting them to Philadelphia, the meeting place, and it was not possible to organize the Convention until May twenty-fifth.[3] From that time until September seventeenth the Convention was in almost daily session, with the exception of ten days of adjournment during which the Committee of Detail was to do its work.[4] A good deal of uncertainty existed among the delegates as to how far they should go in changing the existing form of government. While the majority in the early days of the Convention apparently favored a less centralized form than the one later adopted one point was practically considered an established fact from beginning to end, namely, that the republican form should be continued.[5]

[1]Farrand, *Records of the Federal Convention*, III, 14. (Many of the Farrand references to be used in this chapter could be made to other sources but for the sake of convenience will be confined to the *Records*.)

[2]Rhode Island sent no delegates. See Farrand, *op. cit.*, III, 18.

[3]See quotations from Washington's diary, *ibid.*, III, 20, 21, 26, and letter by King, *ibid.*, III, 26.

[4]Farrand, *op. cit.*, II, 128.

[5]Farrand believes that the New Jersey plan "more nearly represented what most of the delegates supposed that they were sent to do" than did any other plan, and only the fact that it was not presented until the delegates had become ac-

The existence of monarchical tendencies independent of the Constitutional Convention has been considered in the preceding chapter. It has also been asserted both by Americans outside and some within the Convention that there were delegates who cherished monarchical ideas. Jefferson claimed that such delegates had sought to obstruct the progress of the Convention when they foresaw that its work was to be of a republican nature.[6] Luther Martin, a delegate from Maryland, in an address to the legislature of his state, said that while few had openly advocated "one general government . . . of a monarchical nature,"[7] there were "a considerable number," observed by himself "and many others of the convention . . . as being in reality favorers of that sentiment; and, acting upon those principles, covertly endeavouring to carry into effect what they well knew openly and avowedly could not be accomplished."[8] In contrast to this Mr. Baldwin, a delegate from Georgia, after favoring Ezra Stiles with an account "of the whole Progress in Convention" left the latter with the impression that no "Members in Convention had the least Idea of insidiously layg the Founda of a future Monarchy like the European or Asiatic Monarchies either antient or modern. But were unanimously guarded & firm against every Thing of this ultimate Tendency." On the other hand, Mr. Baldwin was later said to be one of those who declared that Hamilton had moved for a "*King, Lords* & Commons." [9]

customed to certain more radical ideas prevented its acceptance. (Farrand, *Framing of the Constitution*, 89.) Compare Fiske, *Critical Period in American History*. See also Mason's statement, May 21, 1787, in Farrand, *Records*, III, 24.

[6]"The Anas," Jefferson, *Writings* (Ford ed.), I, 158. Compare letter written in August, 1787, *ibid.*, IV, 426.

[7]He qualifies the statement by the phrase "under certain restrictions and limitations."

[8]"The Genuine Information . . . Relative to the Proceedings of the . . . Convention;" Farrand, *op. cit.*, III, 179. Connected with this assertion is a similar one involving a list of twenty names of members of the Convention "for a Kingly Government." The tale permits various interpretations. Its importance at this point is merely that according to one account Martin based his charge upon a paper which was of uncertain meaning and which he obtained only indirectly from its author. See *ibid.*, III, 306, 320-324.

[9]E. Stiles, *Diary*, Dec. 21, 1787, quoted in Farrand, *op. cit.*, iii, 169. For Baldwin's connection with the charge against Hamilton see anonymous letter, Aug. 30, 1793. Farrand, *op. cit.*, III, 369.

Some especially unequivocal statements on monarchical tendencies on the eve of the Convention are found among contemporary communications [10]made to the Governor of Canada. "At this moment there is not a gentleman in the States from New Hampshire to Georgia, who does not view the present Government with contempt, who is not convinced of its inefficacy, and who is not desirous of changing it for a monarchy."[11] One class of the people of the States were said (somewhat illogically) to be proposing "a federal Government somewhat resembling the Constitution of the State of New York, with an annual Executive, Senate, and House of Assembly." The second class desired "a sovereign for life with two triennial Houses of Parliament," while the third wished to establish "an Hereditary Monarchy with a form of Government as nearly resembling Great Britain as possible."[12] While many of the first class looked to Washington as a candidate, "those of the second and third . . . cast their eyes to the House of Hanover for a Sovereign" and wished "for one of the King's sons."[13] The third class was described as the ablest and "most powerful" of the three. These monarchists viewed "their own system if successful as affording the fairest prospect of a respectable and stable Government," and had "already fixed upon two gentlemen to go to Great Britain upon this subject, when they judge that matters are ripe for it."[14] They looked forward to the Convention as furnishing them an opportunity "to know fully

[10]These communications were made to Lord Dorchester by his confidential agent in the States. (For an identification of the agent as Major Beckwith and a discussion of his status, see the "Archivist's Report," *Report on Canadian Archives, 1890*, p. xli.) Dorchester forwarded them to Lord Sydney (April 10, 1787) as "Certain Communications of a very interesting nature." The text is printed in *Report on Canadian Archives, 1890*, 97-99.

[11]*Ibid.*, 97.

[12]The following quotations are from the *Report* just cited, page 98, and in keeping with other material in the communications.

[13]*Ibid.*, 98. A later passage in the same paper refers to able men in the States who are "greatly divided in opinion upon this subject, whether they shall raise an American to this dignity, or procure a Sovereign from Great Britain, or from France."

[14]*Ibid.*, 98. It is possible that the writer meant to suggest as one of these Dr. Griffiths of Virginia, described as a friend of Washington and an associate of "men in office, as well as of many respectable individuals in different parts of the country" and as "soon going to England, in hopes of being consecrated a Bishop." *Ibid.*, 99.

each others opinions, to form arrangements and to take such steps as [were] proper to give them effect." The motives for such radical changes were expressed in various terms such as the "unsurmountable" character of the "present public distresses," the fact that the existing federal government was "weakness itself," and they were summed up in the assertion that "the community in general" had been "finding from experience, that a Republican System however beautiful in theory, [was] not calculated for an extensive country."[15]

When the delegates were still arriving, preparatory to the opening of the Convention, George Mason of Virginia confided to his son that there were "some very eccentric opinions" about the work before them, and that "what is a very extraordinary phenomenon, we are likely to find the republicans, on this occasion, issue from the Southern and Middle States, and the anti-republicans from the Eastern." He believed, on second thought, that this was easily explained by the fact that "the people of the Eastern States, setting out with more republican principles, have consequently been more disappointed than we have been."[16] A few days later, after the sessions of the Convention had begun, Mason returned to the subject. "When I first came here, judging from casual conversations with gentlemen from the different States, I was very apprehensive that soured and disgusted with the unexpected evils we had experienced from the democratic principles of our governments, we should be apt to run into the opposite extreme . . . of which I still think there is some danger, though I have the pleasure to find in the convention, many men of fine republican princi-

[15] "Even the Presbyterian Clergy are become Advocates for Monarchy." *Report on Canadian Archives, 1890*, 98.

[16] G. Mason to G. Mason, Jr., May 20, 1787, Farrand, *op. cit.*, III, 23-24. Mason cites "occasional conversations with the deputies of different States, and with some of the general officers of the late army" in Philadelphia "for a general meeting of the Cincinnati" as his only sources of information up to that time. Compare E. Carrington's letter to Jefferson, June 9, 1787, as given in "*Massachusetts Historical Society Proceedings*," 2d ser., XVII. 465. Carrington, writing in New York, the seat of the Continental Congress, declared, "The Eastern opinions are for a total surrender of the State sovereignties, and indeed some amongst them go to a monarchy at once. They have verged to anarchy, while to the southward we have only felt an inconvenience, and their proportionate disposition to an opposite extreme is a natural consequence . . .".

ples."[17] A further statement by Mason on the subject will be noted in a later connection.

The "Pennsylvania Packet" for June 13, 1787, printed an article which had originally appeared 'in a Boston paper. It is doubly significant.[18] It portrays, rather sympathetically, the course of reasoning that had led "men of speculation and refinement"[19] to declare that" a Republican government was impracticable and absurd . . . cursed with inherent inefficiency . . . and that property was more precarious [under it] than under a despot." They had said that a despot "is a man, and would fear the retaliation of his tyranny. But an enthusiastic majority, steeled against compassion, and blind to reason, are equally sheltered form shame and punishment." Thus they had seen "with complacency, the stupid fury of Shays and his banditti, employed to introduce a more stable government whose powers they predicted, would soon be lodged in the hands of abler men. They raved about monarchy, as if we were ripe for it; and as if we were willing to take from the plough-tail or dram shop, some vociferous committee-man, and to array him in royal purple." The author refers to monarchical tendencies in such an assured way that his words rather strengthen a belief that charges were founded on facts.[20] In the second place it is significant that, from the time and place of its second appearance, it would be connected, in the minds of its readers, with the Federal Convention then in session at Philadelphia. The article not only declares "that our king, whenever Providence in its wrath shall send us one, will be a blockhead or a rascal,"[21] but continues with a series of arguments to prove that the United States should not adopt a monarchy. Thus, "The idea of a royal or aristocratic government for America is very absurd. It is repugnant to the genius, and totally incompatible with the cir-

[17]Farrand *op. cit.*, III, 32. Compare letter by W. Grayson, May 24, 1787, *ibid.*, III, 26.

[18]From the *Independent Chronicle* printed at Boston, according to the heading, and signed "Camillus;" *Pennsylvania Packet.* June 13, 1787, p. 2. See also *ibid.*, Jan. 31, 1787, p.2; Feb. 15, 1787, p.3.

[19]They are further characterized as "most sincere lovers of their country" and "not the men to subvert empires."

[20]The idea that the monarchists looked "with complacency" upon the Shays Rebellion would exonerate the Massachusetts Cincinnati from the charge, since they were active in opposing Shays and his forces.

[21]Apparently the writer had in mind some local demagogue rather than a widely admired European prince such as Henry of Prussia.

cumstances of our country. Our interests and our choice have made us republicans—We are too poor to maintain, and too proud to acknowledge a king. The spirit of finance and the ostentation of power would create burdens—These would produce the Shay's and Wheelers'. The army must be augmented—Discontent and oppression would augment of consequence." At this point the writer checked himself, only to start on another line of argument. "But this is mere idle speculation—for every honest man is surely bound to give his support to the existing government until its power becomes intolerable. A change, though for the better, is always to be deplored by the generation in which it is affected. Much is lost, and more is hazarded. Our republic has not yet been allowed a fair trial. The rebellion has called forth its powers and pointed out most clearly the means of giving it stability, let us, therefore, cherish and defend our constitution; and when time and wealth shall have corrupted it, . . . posterity may perform the melancholy task of laying, in human blood and misery, as we have done, the foundation of another government." He concluded with a declaration which was also a reminder and warning: "We who are now upon the stage, bear upon our memories too deep an impression of the miseries of the last revolution to think of attempting another."

A study of the speeches and actions of the delegates does much to determine to what extent they deserved the accusations of Jefferson or needed the advice of "Camillus." Randolph, of Virginia, on June first argued against unity in the executive as "the foetus of monarchy." There may have been an underlying meaning in Wilson's answer that "The people of Amer [ica] did not oppose the British King but the parliament . . . not . . . Unity but a corrupt multitude. . . ."[22] Some days later Mason is reported as asking, "Do gentlemen mean to pave the way to hereditary Monarchy?" and hoping "that nothing like a monarchy would ever be attempted in this Country," for the people never would "consent to such an innovation."[23]

In the meantime Franklin had quite calmly advanced the idea that from the general trend of human affairs the United States would eventually become a monarchy, and that the best that the

[22]Farrand, *op. cit.*, I, 66, 71. Wilson was arguing at the time for a three years term and immediate reëligibility for the chief executive. *Ibid.*, I, 68.

[23]*Ibid.*, I, 101-102.

Convention could do was to postpone the event.[24] Randolph[25] and Mason[26] could not view the situation with such philosophical *sang froid*, and refused to sign the Constitution on the grounds that it would end in "monarchy or a tyrannical aristocracy." The "great diversity of sentiment" in the Convention to which Nicholas Gilman referred July thirty-first, included an advocacy of "high toned Monarchy" by "vigorous minds and warm Constitutions."[27] Elbridge Gerry, on August thirteenth, wrote to General Warren that he sincerely hoped that the proceedings of the Convention, when complete, would "not be engrafted with principles of . . . despotism" which "some, you and I know, would not dislike to find in our national constitution."[28] Nevertheless, about the middle of August, there appeared in a Philadelphia paper an apparently authorized statement which read as follows: "We are informed, that many letters have been written to the members of the foederal convention from different quarters, respecting the reports idly circulating, that it is intended to establish a monarchical government, to send for the bishop of Osnaburgh, &c., &c.—to which it has been uniformly answered, tho' we cannot, affirmatively, tell you what we are doing, we can, negatively, tell you what we are not doing—we never once thought of a king."[29] It is generally conceded that Hamilton's speech of June eighteenth contained the most "monarchical" ideas advanced during the Convention, yet Hamilton later stated that he "never made a proposition in the convention which was not conformable to the republican theory."[30]

[24]Farrand, *op. cit.*, I, 83 ". . . there is a natural inclination in mankind to Kingly Government. It sometimes relieves them from Aristocratic domination. . . . It gives more of the appearance of equality among Citizens, and that they like." Compare Mr. Williamson's remarks, July 24th, i. e., "It was pretty certain he thought that we should at some time or other have a King; but he wished no precaution to be omitted that might postpone the event as long as possible.— Ineligibility a 2d time appeared to him to be the best precaution."

[25]*Ibid.*, II, 564, 631, and Conway, *Edmund Randolph*, 86.

[26]Farrand, *op. cit.*, I, 101, and II, 632.

[27]*Ibid.*, III, 66.

[28]*Ibid.*, III, 69.

[29]From the *Pennsylvania Journal*, August 22nd, *ibid.*, III, 73-74. (The same notice appeared in the *Pennsylvania Packet*, Aug. 20, 1787, p. 3.) Compare A. Martin's letter to Governor Caswell, Aug. 20th, *ibid.*, III, 73. The Bishop of Osnaburgh was the second son of George III.

[30]Extract from J. C. Hamilton, *History of the United States*, Farrand, *op. cit.*, III, 368.

The apparently conflicting statements as to "monarchical" tendencies in the Convention are traceable, at least in part, to differences of definition. Hamilton, in the "Syllabus of the Federalist" emphasized the fact that "republic" had been "used in various senses" and "applied to aristocracies and monarchies," referring to Rome, with its kings; Sparta, with a senate for life; the United Netherlands, with its stadtholder and hereditary nobles; Poland and Great Britain with aristocratic and monarchical institutions.[31] In the Convention he said, "As long as offices are open to all men, and no constitutional rank is established, it is pure republicanism."[32] This concise definition is in no way inconsistent with the longer and more famous one by his one time colleague and later opponent, James Madison.[33]

In his sketchy notes in the "Syllabus of the Federalist" Hamilton said that "monarch" was a term applied to a ruler independent of those governed.[34] In the Convention he said, "*Monarch* is an indefinite term. It marks not either the degree or duration of power. If this Executive Magistrate [the one he had proposed] wd. be a monarch for life—the other propd. [proposed] by the Report from the Committee of the whole, wd. be a monarch for seven years."[35]

Probably many persons at the time considered "monarchy" and "tyranny" as almost interchangeable. Hamilton himself in the first of the two statements just cited [36] was thinking of monarchy in this sense in a style which contrasts with his conception of it when, at other times, he declared the British monarchy

[31] *The Federalist* (Ford ed.), xliii.

[32] Farrand, *op. cit.*,, I 432.

[33] ". . . a government which derives all its powers directly or indirectly from the great body of the people, and is administered by persons holding their offices during pleasure, for a limited period, or during good behavior. It is *essential* to such a government that it be derived from the great body of the society, not from an inconsiderable proportion, or a favored class of it; . . . It is *sufficient* for such a government that the persons administering it be appointed, either directly or indirectly, by the people; and that they hold their appointments by either of the tenures just specified." *The Federalist* (Ford ed.), 246.

[34] *Ibid.*, xliv.

[35] Farrand, *op. cit.*, I, 290.

[36] Compare his warning, ". . . if we incline too much to a democracy, we shall soon shoot into a monarchy." *Ibid.*, I, 432.

to be the best form of government in the world.[37] Paterson of New Jersey, in opposing a measure unfavorable to the small states, said he "had rather submit to a monarch, to a despot, than to such a fate."[38] Wilson recognized and refuted this association of terms by saying, "Where the Executive was really formidable, *King* and *Tyrant*, were naturally associated in the minds of people," but "where the Executive was not formidable" the legislature and tyranny "were most properly associated."[39] In line with this was an assertion made by McClurg of Virginia. He was "not so much afraid of the shadow of monarchy as to be unwilling to approach it; nor so wedded to Republican Govt. as not to be sensible of the tyrannies that had been & may be exercised under that form. It was an essential object with him to make the Executive independent of the Legislature."[40]

It was both asserted[41] and denied[42] that a "unity of the Executive . . . would savor too much of a monarchy." One delegate went so far as to declare that "a single Magistrate . . . will be an elective King, and will feel the spirit of one. He will spare no pains to keep himself in for life, and will then lay a train for the succession of his children."[43]

Many of the delegates apparently regarded long and certain tenure so fundamental a characteristic of monarchy that they refused to adopt a long term of office for the President.[44] Thus Mason "considered an Executive during good behavior as a softer name only for an Executive for life," and warned the assembly that "the next would be an easy step to hereditary Monarchy."[45]

Extensive executive powers spelled monarchy, actual or potential, to the minds of many. Mr. Mason admitted that a monarchy possessed secrecy, dispatch, and energy, the advantages urged for a single executive, "in a much greater degree than a republic."[46] He opposed a complete veto for the executive on the

[37]Farrand, *op. cit.*, I, 288.
[38]*Ibid.*, I, 179.
[39]*Ibid.*, II, 300-301. Compare his words on June 16th, *ibid.*, I, 254.
[40]*Ibid.*, II, 36.
[41]As by Randolph. See *ibid.*, I, 74.
[42]As by Wilson. See *ibid.*, I, 66, 74.
[43]Mr. Williamson of North Carolina. *Ibid.*, II, 101.
[44]See *ibid.*, II, 35-36.
[45]*Ibid.*, II, 35.
[46]*Ibid.*, I, 112.

grounds that it would tend to constitute a monarchy more dangerous than the British Government—"an elective one."[47] Mr. Rutledge "was by no means disposed to grant so great a power" as the appointment of judges "to any single person" because, as he said, "The people will think we are leaning too much towards Monarchy."[48] Gerry opposed the appointment of the senate by the national executive as "a stride towards monarchy that few will think of!"[49] The monarchical character of the war powers of the executive did not elude Charles Pinckney's watchful eye. Powers of peace and war in the executive "would render the Executive a Monarchy, of the worst kind, towit an elective one."[50]

With these ideas as to what the members of the Convention did or did not consider monarchical characteristics one may the more profitably consider the so-called Hamilton plan.[51] Its monarchical character is largely a matter of definition.[52]

It will be recalled that Hamilton denied having made any "proposition to the convention which was not conformable to the republican theory."[53] Yet, according to Madison's notes, Hamilton "acknowledged himself not to think favorably of Republican Government" and "addressed his remarks to those who think favorably of it, in order to prevail on them to tone their Government as high as possible."[54] The conflict of ideas in Hamilton's mind may well be summed up in his own words, "I fear Republicanism will not answr. [answer] and yet we cannot go beyond it."[55] Hamilton felt that one branch of the government could well be especially devoted to the representation of the "poorer order of citizens."[56] His plan provided for an assembly elected by the

[47]Farrand, *op. cit.*, I, 101.

[48]*Ibid.*, I, 119.

[49]*Ibid.*, I, 152.

[50]*Ibid.*, I, 64-65. Compare Randolph's statement, *ibid.*, II, 67.

[51]This formed the chief part of a speech which he made in the Convention June 18th. See *ibid.*, I, 282-293. See also his remarks June 26th, *ibid.*, I, 424, 432.

[52]See interpretations by Farrand, *Framing of the Constitution* 88; Von Holst, *History of the United States*, I, 111; Krauel, "Prince Henry of Prussia", *American Historical Review*, XVII, 50.

[53]Above, p. 82.

[54]Farrand, *op. cit.*, I, 424.

[55]*Ibid.*, I, 303.

[56]*Ibid.*, I, 424.

people, "on a broad foundation."[57] He did not propose, however, that the only check on the democratic assembly was to be in a democratic senate and a democratic chief magistrate. Thus he proposed that "one body of the legislature be constituted during good behavior or life" and that the executive have a similar tenure.[58] The vast extent of the country "almost led him to despair" of the establishment of a republican government.[59] His expedient against the operation of centrifugal forces was to have the national executive appoint the state governors and to give to these latter an absolute veto over the state legislatures.[60] This he considered not unrepublican since the national executive himself received his election, though indirectly, from the people.[61] Much has been made of Hamilton's expressed preference for the British constitution.[62] He declared he would "go to the full length of republican principles" in order to approach as near as possible to "the excellency of the British executive."[63] But Hamilton was not a man to make any government an end in itself. He wished to approach the British form because he was convinced that "nothing short of such an executive can be efficient."[64] Hamilton, under the existing circumstances, did not even desire to transfer the British monarchical form intact to American soil. He believed at this time a maxim he later expressed by saying that "what may be good at Philadelphia, may be bad at Paris, and ridiculous at Petersburgh,"[65] a formula which, of course, could be reversed and made to include London. His real desire seems to have been to combine the separation of powers and the stability of the British form with the representative feature of a republic

[57]Farrand, *op. cit.*, II, 553-554, I, 291.

[58]*Ibid.*, I, 300.

[59]*Ibid.*, I, 288.

[60]*Ibid.*, I, 293.

[61]See *ibid.*, I, 292. Compare *Journal of the Convention*, 113. The "good behavior" members of the national legislature were to be chosen by electors. Farrand, *op. cit.*, I, 291.

[62]See, for examples, *ibid.*, I, 288-289, and Jefferson, *Writings* (Ford ed.), I, 166; IX, 295; X, 34.

[63]Farrand, *op. cit.*, I, 299-300.

[64]*Ibid.*, i, 299.

[65]Letter to La Fayette, Jan. 6, 1799; Hamilton, *Works* (J. C. Hamilton ed.), VI, 388.

and the popular participation consistent with democracy, and thus to meet the peculiar needs of America.

The form of government described by Hamilton might well appear a sort of elective monarchy or stadtholdership and as such immediately antagonize his fellow citizens. Aside from the very general prejudice in America against such forms, due to an exaltation of republican theory, the unhappy experiences of the Dutch with their stadtholder and the Poles with their elective monarch were well known.[66] Yet there are grounds on which to take issue with the conclusion that Hamilton presented his views with no further hope nor purpose than to counterbalance the New Jersey plan and to reach a happy medium between the two.[67] Hamilton[68] "hoped Gentlemen of different opinions would bear with him . . and recollect the change of opinion on this subject which had taken place and was still going on." He reminded them that it "was once thought that the power of Congs [Congress] was amply sufficient to secure the end of their institution. The error was now seen by every one . . . This progress . . . led him to anticipate the time, when others as well as himself would join" in the assertion that the British Government was the only one in the world which united "public strength with individual security."

John Adams was always sure that his "Defence of the Constitutions of the United States," which reached America and was republished there on the eve of the Convention[69] did much to make the Convention a success.[70] Despite its later unpopularity as "monarchical" propaganda[71] the book was certainly well received at first.[72] The comparative readiness of most of the delegates to be guided by the "long experience" of the mother coun-

[66]See Farrand, *op. cit.*, I, 90, 92, 102-103, n., 326-327, 449, 476; II, 9, 31, 67-68, 202, 541; and I, 290-291, 459; II, 30, 31, 109-110.

[67]See Farrand, *Framing of the Constitution*, 87, 89.

[68]According to Madison's record of his speech on June 18th, Farrand, *Records*, I, 288.

[69]See *Massachusetts Historical Society Collections*, 5th ser., IV, 332; Jay, *Correspondence*, III, 247.

[70]See John Adams's recital of testimonials to this effect by Mr. Dickinson, Governor Martin, and others. *Massachusetts Historical Society Collections*, 5th ser., IV, 332-333.

[71]*Massachusetts Historical Society Proceedings*, 2d ser., XV, 118-119; C. F. Adams, *Life of John Adams*, 433.

[72]*Massachusetts Historical Society Proceedings*, 2d ser. XV, 118; Jay, *Correspondence*, III, 251; Jefferson, *Works* (Washington ed.), II, 128.

try[73] was founded on the Americans' familiarity with Blackstone, Montesquieu, and Locke,[74] as well as with their practical experience under the type of government portrayed by them. But Adams's presentation of the old ideas came at a psychological moment, and must have been effective in promoting the change of opinion which Hamilton believed he observed. The "Defence" praised the British constitution to an extent to satisfy the heart of Hamilton himself.

Some of the delegates who agreed with Hamilton in dreading too much democracy were such strong believers in states' rights as to be out of sympathy with Hamilton's entirely nationalistic plan.[75] But there were others in the convention who very likely were deterred from full sympathy with Hamilton's plan by the one fear of risking "what was then deemed the last chance for a respectable union, on a scheme which would be hopeless of acceptance."[76] A survey of the position of these men will follow.[77]

It has been said that John Dickinson "frankly joined that minority which was outspoken in its belief in a monarchy—an action that comported with his refusal to sign the Declaration of Independence and his reluctance to embark upon the stormy sea of Revolution."[78] Not long after the opening of the Convention he remarked "that a firm Executive could only exist in a limited Monarchy . . . A limited Monarchy he considered as *one* of the best Governments in the world. . . . It was certain that equal blessings had never yet been derived from any of the republican form."[79] But he perceived that a "limited monarchy was out of the question," because of the "spirit of the times" and the "state of our affairs," and because it was impossible to create "by a stroke of the pen" a "House of Nobles," which he considered essential to this form of government. He therefore looked to remedying the republican form in such a way as to make it more perfect than

[73]See "Great Britain" in "General Index," Farrand, *op. cit.*, III, 661.

[74]See *New International Encyclopaedia*, III, 363; XVI, 198; XIV, 276.

[75]H. C. Lodge, *Alexander Hamilton*, 61.

[76]*Ibid.*, 61.

[77]In the present chapter the writer has used parts of several chapters in her earlier (unprinted) thesis in which a study was made of "Monarchical Tendencies in the United States from 1782 to 1787."

[78]C. A. Beard, *Economic Interpretation of the Constitution*, 194.

[79]Farrand, *op. cit.*, I, 86-87. Reread comments on Dickinson's views on government, above, p. 19.

it had proved to be in the republics of the ancient world.[80] He doubtless voted for a good behavior tenure for the executive as a means to this end.[81]

Gorham's attitude towards monarchy at the time of the Convention is of peculiar interest in view of his supposed connection with the Prince Henry of Prussia affair. His only reference to monarchy, so far as we can learn from the records, was made in supporting the proposal that the central government should guarantee a republican constitution to each state. He observed that it would be strange that the general government should "be restrained from interposing" to subdue any rebellion that might take place in a state, for "At this rate an enterprising Citizen might erect the standard of Monarchy in a particular State, might gather together partizans from all quarters, might extend his views from State to State, and threaten to establish a tyranny over the whole."[82] His manner of speaking indicates that he considered an attempt at monarchy by no means impossible or impracticable but does not suggest any sympathy with the idea. It does, however, suggest something as to the course that might once have been considered in connection with the "monarchical plot" of the preceding year.

Rufus King, whatever may have been his attitude towards a proposal for importing a foreign prince, certainly favored the strongest proposals made in the Convention. He was one of the three delegates who, on June fourth, voted for a complete negative for the executive.[83] On June first he upheld a seven year term[84] for this official and later, when this term was negatived, he expressed anxiety lest too short a term be adopted.[85] On July twentieth he is reported as saying that the executive "ought not to be impeachable unless he hold his office during good behavior, a tenure which would be most agreeable to him; provided an independent and effectual forum could be devised" for impeachment.[86] On the other hand, his suggestion on July twenty-fourth, that the execu-

[80]Farrand, *op. cit.*, I, 87.
[81]*Ibid.*, II, 36.
[82]July 18, 1787, *ibid* II, 48.
[83]*Ibid.*, I, 108.
[84]*Ibid.*, I, 72.
[85]July 19th, *ibid.*, II, 59.
[86]*Ibid.*, II, 67.

tive term be twenty years, since "This is the medium life of princes," is noted by Madison as "possibly . . . meant as a caricature" of the immediately preceding suggestions for terms of eleven and fifteen years.[87] Hamilton felt sure that King understood his point of view for during his absence from the Convention, in the latter part of August, it was King whom he asked to keep him informed of any new developments.[88]

A motion for a good behavior term for the executive was made on July seventeenth by James McClurg of Virginia.[89] His expressed object was to make this official independent of the legislature.[90] Mr. Broom of Delaware "highly approved" the good behavior motion.[91] Apparently neither of these men was an effective speaker or particularly influential in the Convention.[92]

Hamilton later pointed out that Madison voted for the "highest toned" feature he had proposed.[93] Not only did Madison vote for good behavior tenure for the executive[94] but he supported it, with considerable caution,[95] during the debates. But in a footnote he explained, "This vote is not to be considered as any certain index of opinion, as a number in the affirmative probably had it chiefly in view to alarm those attached to a dependence of the Executive on the Legislature, & thereby facilitate some final arrangement of a contrary tendency."[96] As he said in "The Federalist," Madison was convinced that "no other form [than a Republic] would be reconcilable with the genius of . . . America; with the . . . principles of the Revolution; or with that . . . determination which animates every votary of freedom to rest all

[87]Farrand, *op. cit.*, II, 102 and n.

[88]*Ibid.*, III, 70. Note that King was later a leader of the Nationalistic party. *New International Encyclopaedia*, XIII, 241.

[89]Farrand, *op. cit.*, II, 33.

[90]*Ibid.*, II, 36.

[91]*Ibid.*, II, 33.

[92]See Pierce, "Character Sketches," *ibid.*, III, 95, 93.

[93]*Ibid.*, III, 368-369, 398.

[94]*Ibid.*, II, 36.

[95]For example he recorded that his support of McClurg's motion was due to his "particular regard" for the mover *Ibid.*, II,34-35. See his remarks on impeachment on the same occasion.

[96]*Ibid.*, II, 36. Six states voted in the affirmative, four in the negative.

our political experiments on the capacity of mankind for self-government."[97]

At the time when Gouverneur Morris was named minister to France George Mason deprecated his appointment on the grounds of Morris's political heresy. ". . . in his place, as a Member of the federal Convention in philadelphia," wrote Mason, "I heard him express the following Sentiment.—'we must have a Monarch sooner or later.' [tho' I think his word was a *Despot*] 'and the sooner we take him, while we are able to make a Bargain with him, the better."[98] Yet in debate Morris declared himself "as little a friend to monarchy as any gentlemen. He concurred . . . that the way to keep out monarchical Govt. was to establish such a Republ Govt. as wd. make the people happy and prevent a desire of change.[99] It is difficult to discover what means this "fickle and inconstant"[100] delegate really favored as attaining this end. On July sixth he said, "We should either take the British Constitution altogether or make one for ourselves."[101] On July seventeenth he seconded McClurg's motion for a good behavior tenure, expressed "great pleasure" at hearing of "so valuable an ingredient," and was even "indifferent how the Executive should be chosen, provided he held his place by this tenure."[102] This was at a time when the appointment of the executive was to be by the legislature. Two days later he was advocating election by the people and a two year term.[103] Earlier in the Convention Morris had approved a life tenure for the Senate and appointment of senators by the executive.[104]

[97]*The Federalist* (Ford ed.), 245. For further remarks by Madison on monarchy see Farrand, *op. cit.*, I, 70; II, 35.

[98]Mason to Monroe, Jan. 30, 1792. *Monroe Papers*. Manuscripts Division, Library of Congress.

[99]Farrand, *op. cit.*, II, 35-36.

[100]Pierce, "Character Sketches," *ibid.*, III, 92.

[101]*Ibid.*, I, 545.

[102]*Ibid.*, II, 33.

[103]*Ibid.*, II, 54. The direct reason for this stand was his desire to avoid impeachments. Morris believed a two year term would in fact be indefinitely extended so long as the magistrate "should behave himself well." *Ibid.*, II, 54. The good behavior tenure had been voted down in the meantime.

[104]*Ibid.*, I, 512-513.

Read of Delaware, though from a small state, favored a strong national government,[105] appointment of the Senate by the chief executive[106] and absolute negative for the executive,[107] and a good behavior tenure for the Senate.[108] His delegation voted for a good behavior tenure for the executive.[109]

Finally, the question may arise as to whether Hamilton expected support from Washington. Although Hamilton quite possibly knew of the outcome of the Nicola affair, he may have had reason to believe that Washington had been gradually tending towards stronger measures.[110] At any rate, his expectation that, although he had not compared his ideas with Washington, the latter would receive them with courteous consideration,[111] was not disappointed. The answer to Hamilton's letter of July 3d reveals sympathy and understanding on the part of Washington, who thanked the former for his letter, and wished that he were back in the Convention, since the crisis was "important and alarming." Washington almost despaired "of seeing a favorable issue to the proceedings of our convention," felt contempt for "narrow-minded" men who opposed a "strong and energetic government," and believed that their contention that the people would not accede to the form proposed was only an excuse for their opposition. Most important of all is his conclusion that "admitting that the present sentiment is as they prognosticate, the proper question ought nevertheless to be, Is it, or is it not the best form that such a country as this can adopt?"[112] As presiding officer of the Convention Washington had little opportunity to express his views on the points at issue.

We have said that Hamilton's proposals were the most "monarchical" of any made in the Convention and that while not voted

[105]Farrand, *op. cit.*, I, 136, 202, 463.

[106]*Ibid.*, I, 151.

[107]*Ibid.*, II, 200.

[108]*Ibid.*, I, 409-421.

[109]*Ibid.*, II, 36. He was later reputed a "monarchist" by some persons in his home state. See Rodney, *Diary*, Mar. 22, 1801. Manuscripts Division, Library of Congress.

[110]Such a tendency is suggested by a study of Washington's correspondence from July, 1786, through March, 1787. Washington, *Writings* (Ford ed.), XI. See above page 57.

[111]Hamilton to Washington, July 3, 1787, *Works* (J. C. Hamilton ed.), I, 436.

[112]July 10, 1787, Washington, *Writings* (Ford ed.), XI, 162.

upon as a whole some parts appeared as motions and received considerable support. Hamilton professed to believe that popular opinion might also come to support such ideas. In his speech of June eighteenth he declared that "a great progress [had] been already made" and was "still going on in the public mind." This led him to believe that in time the people would be "unshackled from their prejudices," and "be ready to go as far at least" as he proposed.[113] A fortnight later, in his passage through the Jerseys, he believed he saw evidence that an "astonishing revolution" had already taken place in the minds of the people, and that they had come to desire "something not very remote from that which they had lately quitted." He wrote, "These appearances, though they will not warrant a conclusion that the people are yet ripe for such a plan as I advocate, yet serve to prove that there is no reason to despair of their adopting one equally energetic, if the Convention should think proper to propose it."[114] Jefferson later asserted that the monarchical ideas of Hamilton and other delegates, being noised abroad among the people, were responsible for their "strong opposition to the conventional Constitution."[115] But Jefferson's prejudice against his great opponent may have colored his impressions just as Hamilton's prejudice in favor of his own views may have lent his impressions a rosy tinge. The truth seems to be that public opinion of the period was relatively unformed and unfathomable. Contemporary observations on political movements were chiefly confined to the writings of political leaders who in that day, far more than now, formed a class distinct from their constituents. When we seek to know the public mind through the delegates' impressions of it we are again baffled, for these impressions were often contradictory. Madison was not alone in his assertion that it was impossible to know the public will on the object of the Convention.[116] Wilson sensibly pointed out the danger that the sentiments of "the particular circle in which one moved," be "mistaken for the general voice."[117]

[113]Farrand, *op. cit.*, I, 291.

[114]Letter to Washington, July 3, 1787, Hamilton, *Works* (J. C. Hamilton ed.), I, 435-436; (Lodge ed., VIII, 175-176).

[115]Jefferson, *Writings* (Ford ed.), I, 159.

[116]Farrand, *op. cit.*, I, 215.

[117]*Ibid.*, I, 253.

While professing that the people's opinions could not be known on particular points, Madison was convinced that "In general they believe there is something wrong in the present system that requires amendment," and that if the Convention's plan should fail the people, in despair, would "incline to Monarchy."[118] Gerry, on the contrary, held that the mere savour of despotism would alarm the people.[119] Mason admitted that "the mind of the people of America, as elsewhere, was unsettled as to some points" but insisted it was "settled as to others," one of which was "an attachment to republican Government." The basis of his conclusion was the general agreement of the state constitutions in the matter.[120] Mr. Gerry did not hesitate to announce, " There were not $\frac{1}{1000}$ part of our fellow citizens who were not agst. every approach towards Monarchy."[121]

Hamilton's notes for June 1st include a clear and interesting outline of Randolph's speech of that date. The part pertaining to public opinion is as follows:

"I Situation of this Country peculiar ——

II — Taught the people an aversion to Monarchy

III All their Constitutions opposed to it ——

IV — Fixed character of the people opposed to it ——

V — If proposed 'twill prevent a fair discussion of the plan."[122]

The situation, as it appeared to Madison, is summed up in his letter to Jefferson of September 6th, as follows:

"Nothing can exceed the universal anxiety for the event of the meeting here. Reports and conjectures abound concerning the nature of the plan which is to be proposed. The public however is certainly in the dark with regard to it.[123] The Convention is equally in the dark as to the reception wch. may be given to it on its publication. All the prepossessions are on the right side, but

[118]Farrand, *op. cit.*, I, 220-221.

[119]*Ibid.*, I, 220.

[120]*Ibid.*, I, 339.

[121]*Ibid.*, I, 425.

[122]*Ibid.*, I, 72.

[123]The lady who is reported by McHenry to have asked Franklin ,"Well Doctor what have we got a republic or a monarchy?" was certainly "in the dark." Her question, however, betrays no special anxiety. *Ibid.*, III, 85.

it may well be expected that certain characters will wage war against any reform whatever.[124]

There were two classes among the people who, more than any others, were said to entertain thoughts of monarchical government for the United States. These were the Cincinnati and the Loyalists. The most definite charge against the former was probably that made by M. Otto, French chargé d' affaires at New York. He reported that the Cincinnati were "interested in the establishment of a solid government" since under a feeble one they had not received their pay. Their desire was to consolidate the states and to "place at their head . . . Washington with all the prerogatives of a crowned head." This they threatened to do by force as soon as they should be "convinced of the futility of the *Convention.*" Otto considered this project entirely absurd because of the feebleness and unpopularity of the Cincinnati.[125]

The charge connected with the Loyalists had wider connections, being bound up with the belief in some quarters, that the Convention might set up a monarchical government and invite a British prince to the throne. These rumors became so current in the midsummer of 1787, and members of the Convention were so plied with questions about it that an unofficial, but seemingly authorized, denial was inserted in a Philadelphia paper.[126] A similar report, circulating in Europe, was indignantly denied by William Short[127] an American living in Paris. Short ridiculed the charge as being as incredible as a report would be which claimed that the English people, weary of existing burdens and disturbances, wished to "return under the dominion of the Dukes of Normandy . . . & had solicited the King of France to take them under his protection . . . " He based his denial in part upon the fact that "nothing of the sort had been heard of within any part of the

[124]These were the men holding state offices under the Articles of Confederation. See Hamilton's letter to Washington, July 3, 1787, Hamilton, *Works* (Lodge ed.), VIII, 175. Madison's letter to Jefferson is in Farrand, *op. cit.*, III, 77-78.

[125]Written in New York, June 10, 1787, by M. Otto to Count de Montmorin, secretary of state for foreign affairs. Farrand, *op. cit.*, III, 43-44. Otto's suspicions may have been aroused by the presence of numerous members of the society at Philadelphia at the time of the Constitutional Convention. They were, however, attending their own regular convention.

[126]Above, page 82, n. 29.

[127]On Short's career abroad see *Appletons' Cyclopaedia of American Biography*, V, 516.

United States, judging by letters he had received from that country as late as September nineth of that year [1787]."[128] Short could not have made this last statement the following summer for by that time he must have received the statement by Crèvecoeur that "a very large number of persons" in New England "would like to return to English domination."[129] In fact, by the opening of the new year (1788) Short's American correspondents had led him to believe that astounding strides "towards a toleration of Monarchical" principles had already been made.[130] That similar reports received credence in British official circles is certain. Lord Sydney, writing at Whitehall, September 14, 1787, addressed Lord Dorchester as follows:

"The report of an intention on the part of America to apply for a sovereign of the house of Hanover has circulated here;[131] and should an application of that nature be made, it will require a very nice consideration in what manner so important a subject should be treated. But whatever ideas may have been formed upon it, it will upon all accounts be advisable that any influence which your lordship may possess should be exerted to discourage the strengthening their alliance with the house of Bourbon, which must naturally follow were a sovereign to be chosen from any branch of that family."[132]

Late in 1788 Lord Dorchester enclosed a memorandum of the Federal Convention in a letter to Lord Sydney. It mentioned

[128]Letter of Oct. 15, 1787, *William Short Papers*. Manuscripts Division, Library of Congress.

[129]Described above, p. 71.

[130]This is indicated in Short's letter of January 31st, quoted below, page 100.

[131]Franklin, in France in 1785, wrote that Britain was circulating there tales of distress in America and desire for a "restoration of the old Government." [Letter to Jay, Feb. 8; Franklin, *Writings* (Smyth ed.) IX, 287-288.] For specimen of a similar tale in America see *Pennsylvania Packet*, Jan. 8, 1787, p. 2. Prince William Henry (not the "Bishop of Osnaburgh") apparently visited America late in 1786, judging by a newspaper item of his arrival at Halifax. (*Ibid.*, Oct. 31, 1786, p. 2.) The military preparedness of Canada under Lord Dorchester was stressed in a newspaper article, June 23, 1787. (*Ibid.*, p. 3.)

[132]Farrand, *op. cit.*, III, 80-81. This suggests that Lord Sydney gave considerable weight to Lord Dorchester's enclosure of April 10th. See above, p. 78. A somewhat similar communication of a later year may be found below, page 105.

"Colonel Hamilton's" plan, "that had in view the establishment of a monarchy, and the placing the crown upon the head of a foreign prince, which was overruled, although supported by some of the ablest members of the convention."[133]

A letter of this general type, circulating in Connecticut, apparently in July and August, 1787, greatly interested Alexander Hamilton. He set on foot an investigation of its source and reception.[134] Colonel Humphreys reported that the letter had been "received and circulated with avidity" by the Loyalists "whether it was fabricated by them or not." He further declared that "the quondam Tories" had "undoubtedly conceived hopes of a future union with G. Britain, from the inefficiency of our Government." He had seen a letter, written at the time of the tumults in Massachusetts the preceding winter, "stating the impossibility of our being happy under our present Constitution, and proposing . . . that the efforts of the moderate, the virtuous, and the brave, should be exerted to effect a reunion with the parent State. He mentioned, among other things, how instrumental the Cincinnati might be, and how much it would redound to their emolument."[135] Even if Humphreys' report was faithful to the facts the sentiment of the "quondam Tories" was not an effective factor so soon after the War. It will be recalled that thousands of them had left the country and that those who remained were in no position to put their ideas into effect. Hamilton, in September, 1787, said a reunion with Great Britain was "not impossible, though not much to be feared." He thought the "most plausible shape . . . would be the establishment of a son of the present monarch . . . with a family compact."[136] Later he pointed out the probability that such a compact would be opposed to the point of war by France, as too greatly increasing British resources. He added that the Americans would soon regain their independence, in any case.[137]

[133]Enclosed in letter of date Oct. 14, 1788, Farrand, *op. cit.*, III, 354. The letters of Phineas Bond, British consul at Philadelphia in 1787, appear to contain no similar report. See, for example, his letters of July 2 and September 20, 1787, *American Historical Association Report, 1896*, I, 539, 546.

[134]Hamilton, *Works* (J. C. Hamilton ed.), I, 440.

[135]*Ibid.*, I, 442-443.

[136]"Impressions as to the new constitution (Sept. 1787)," Hamilton, *Works* (Lodge ed.), I, 402.

[137]"Americanus" (Feb., 1794), *ibid.*, IV, 277-279.

The proposed Constitution was made public in September when the Convention completed its work. Its reception by the public and the charges of "monarchism" against its first administrators will be considered in the following chapter.

CHAPTER VI

MONARCHICAL TENDENCIES IN THE UNITED STATES FROM THE CLOSE OF THE CONSTITUTIONAL CONVENTION TO 1801

During the sharply contested movement for ratification the Constitution was attacked from some quarters as a monarchical instrument.[1] Thus George Mason, in the Virginia convention, advocating rotation in office for the presidency, said, " . . . as it now stands, he may continue in office for life; or, in other words, it will be an elective monarchy."[2] His colleague, James Monroe, agreed with him,[3] while William Grayson thought such continuance "highly probable."[4] Earlier in the convention Patrick Henry had delivered his famous denunciation of the Constitution, namely, that "among other deformities . . . it squints towards monarchy." He had gone on to say, "If your American chief be a man of ambition and abilities, how easy is it for him to render himself absolute! The army is in his hands, and if he be a man of address, it will be attached to him, and it will be the subject of long meditation with him to seize the first auspicious moment to accomplish his design."[5] Mr. Lowndes, in the South Carolina convention, declared, "On the whole, this was the best preparatory plan for a monarchical government he had read." It "came so near" to the British form that, "as to our changing from a republic to a monarchy, it was what everybody must naturally expect."[6]

[1]This was not a surprise to the framers, according to James Wilson, who said, "It was expected by many, that the cry would have been against the powers of the President as a monarchical power." Elliot, *Debates on the Federal Constitution*, II, 511.

[2]*Ibid.*, III, 485.

[3]*Ibid.*, III, 489.

[4]*Ibid.*, III, 491.

[5]*Ibid.*, III, 58-59. Grayson, Monroe, and Mason had noted foreign intermeddling as an important factor in the situation.

[6]*Ibid.*, IV, 311. See also Maclaine, in North Carolina convention (*ibid.*, IV, 135) and, in contrast, Smith, in Massachusetts convention (*ibid.*, II, 102-103).

The private correspondence of the time contains some similar expressions. The wide circulation of such fears is suggested by the recognition of them by Edward Carrington of Virginia, writing in New York,[7] and William Plumer, writing in New Hampshire.[8] Richard Henry Lee, addressing Samuel Adams, denounced the proposed system as "elective despotism," and remarked that chains were still chains, "whether made of gold or iron."[9] William Short, following American developments from his residence in France, wrote to a friend in London that the proposed constitution "has converted the thirteen republics into one mixed monarchy—for notwithstanding the humble title of President elective from four years to four years, he will have greater powers than several monarchs have." He feared not so much the immediate danger as that "the President of the eighteenth century" would "form a stock on which will be engrafted a King in the nineteenth."[10] In January, 1788, Short declared to Grayson that "the proposed Constitution" and "a great part of what is written on it" led him to believe that "the Citizens of America [had] made in three years, larger strides towards a toleration of monarchical principles than it had been supposed possible they should have made in as many centuries."[11] His friend Nelson, in a letter written at Williamsburgh, in March of that year, cited foreign precedents to prove that the presidency would become an hereditary office. He believed he would accept the Constitution without hesitation could the president become ineligible for

[7]To Jefferson, Oct. 23, 1787, *Massachusetts Historical Society Proceedings*, 2d ser., XVII, 482.

[8]To D. Tilton, Dec. 16, 1787, *William Plumer Letters*. Manuscripts Division, Library of Congress.

[9]Oct. 5, 1787, *Letters of R. H. Lee* (J. C. Ballagh ed.), II, 445.

[10]Short to J. Cutting, Nov. 15, 1787, *William Short Papers*. Manuscripts Division, Library of Congress. Short was in close communication with Jefferson at this time. Another American on the Continent, Bishop by name, professed to be so apprehensive that the Constitution would be ratified that he frequently dreamed of being a slave. He suspected that the Constitution was "only a Trojan Horse." (Letter to Short, Amiens, Jan. 31, 1788, *William Short Papers*.) The unscrupulous character of the man makes the words of little consequence, except as a picturesque statement, or perhaps parody, of the fears of his correspondent.

[11]Jan. 31, 1788, *ibid*. Compare with Grayson to Short, Nov. 10, 1787, *Ibid*.

reëlection.[12] But elaborate arguments[13] were brought to bear upon such men. Later, after the acceptance of a bill of rights was assured,[14] they became supporters of the Constitution, although the first ten amendments did not meet their objections in regard to the office of president.

In curious contrast to this antimonarchical opposition to the proposed Constitution stands a group of negotiations, along the frontiers, professedly looking to friendly monarchies for aid and patronage as a remedy for republican neglect. These projects, at one time or another, involved to some noticeable extent Vermont, Kentucky, Tennessee (the last only incidentally), and the settlements northwest of the Ohio river.[15] The most outstanding as well as the most baffling of them all involves James Wilkinson and other leading Kentuckians on the one side, and the officials of His Most Catholic Majesty of Spain on the other.[16]

While the Convention at Philadelphia was devoting the midsummer days of 1787 to the framing of an improved constitution for the United States, James Wilkinson was drafting a memorial[17] to the Spanish Government. Wilkinson's prestige and influence

[12]Mar. 13, 1788, *William Short Papers.*

[13]Such as J. B. Cutting's long and interesting letter of Dec. 13, 1787. Cutting, among other things, declared the American Senate and House had enough power to balance even an hereditary President, and labored long to show that the President's power was small as compared with that of the British King. *Ibid.* See also pamphlet by T. Coxe in support of the Constitution, *An Examination of the Constitution.*

[14]See letters by Short, Mar. 16, 1788 and Jan. 28, 1790, by Cutting, Feb. [5] 1790, by Nelson, July 12, 1788 and Dec. 17, 1789, William *Short Papers*; by Benjamin Franklin, Oct. 22, Oct. 24, 1788, *Writings* (Smyth ed.), IX, 665-666, 676. Compare Von Holst, *History of the United States*, I, 65.

[15]Georgia seems to have been but slightly involved, if at all. See, however, references by Lieutenant Governor Simcoe (of Canada) to dealings with General Elijah Clark of Georgia. *Report on Canadian Archives, 1891,* Upper Canada, p. 3. See also *American Historical Review,* XXI, 552, where S. F. Bemis points out these relations developed "in the period between [Clarke's] first disappointment over President Washington's Creek treaty of 1790. . . and his relations with Genet in 1793 and trans-Oconee outbreak of 1794."

[16]Typical accounts of the Wilkinson Conspiracy and its background are found in H. Marshall, *History of Kentucky*, II, 188-189; I, 270, 282, 313; T. M. Green, *The Spanish Conspiracy*, 120-138, 149ff; R. M. McElroy, *Kentucky in the Nation's History*, 120-121, 131-136, 165 n. 2; N. S. Shaler, *Kentucky*, 98, 101, 137, 139. *The American Historical Review,* IX, 490-506, 749-766, contains some helpful accounts.

[17]This first memorial was dated August 21, 1787. *American Historical Review,* IX, 748.

among the frontiersmen[18] entitles his propositions to some consideration. The substance of them was as follows: First, the Spanish king "should receive the inhabitants of the Kentucky region as subjects and take them and their territory under his protection;" and second, "the inhabitants of Kentucky and the other settlements [along the rivers] emptying into the Ohio, who might desire to emigrate to Louisiana should be allowed to settle in that province."[19]

The Spanish Council of State, late in the following year,[20] formulated a reply which undertook to encourage the immigration plan but not the more radical part of the memorial, since it was deemed "unadvisable" to consider the latter "until the Kentuckians attain the independence from the United States to which they aspire, although they should not be suffered to lose hope that in case of success they would be admitted [as subjects] . . ."[21] These sentiments in the main pleased Wilkinson, according to his second memorial (September 17, 1789),[22] since, as he said, recent changes in the United States[23] made immediate annexation impossible. However, he urged that the Spanish government grant such favorable commercial concessions to the western Americans as to win their friendship and confidence and thus pave the way for an ultimate political connection. In case such a connection should be made Wilkinson stipulated that Kentucky should enjoy "the right of local self-government".[24] The far-reaching scope of the plan, geographically considered, is to be inferred from its author's plea that "secret and indirect agencies" should be employed to "accomplish the above-mentioned separation and independence from the United States," and that "such a condition of affairs should not be confined to this region

[18]For a concise summary of Wilkinson's activities, questionable and otherwise, see Channing, *The Jeffersonian System*, 156. See also Shaler, *Kentucky*, 98, and especially McElroy, *op. cit.*, 115-116.

[19]This summary is the one included in the written decision of the Spanish Council of State. *American Historical Review*, IX, 749.

[20]November 20, 1788. Approved by the King December 1, 1788. *Ibid.*, IX, 749-750.

[21]*Ibid.*, IX, 749.

[22]The second memorial is printed in *ibid.*, IX, 751-764.

[23]I. e., the establishment of a new government under the federal constitution of 1787.

[24]*American Historical Review*, IX, 751.

[Kentucky] alone, but should be set up more or less in all the settlements along the Ohio. . . ."[25]

It will be recalled that Wilkinson later won acquittal from charges of disloyalty to the United States government. He then described his representations to Spain as wholly insincere and merely means to the end of winning commercial concessions for himself and his fellow Kentuckians.[26]

If this be true, Wilkinson's earlier assertions that a group of leading westerners of his region were ready to help him bring Kentucky under the Spanish flag (in return for due commercial and other gains)[27] must be discounted equally with his own oath of allegiance to Spain.[28] On which occasion, if either, Wilkinson spoke the truth, whether or not any economic lure was powerful enough to lead American frontiersmen to bow down to an alien monarchy,[29] are the only questions connected with the compli-

[25]*American Historical Review*, IX, 753. Compare *ibid.*, 754, 755-756. Wilkinson mentions by name the "settlements of Cumberland, Franklin, Holstein [editor's note "Holston?"], New River, Green Briar, Tiger's Valley, Monongahela, Alleghany, and the settlements now forming to the northwest of the Ohio on the rivers Muskingum and Miami." *Ibid.*, IX, 755-756. An especially definite reference to the last two named is found in Wilkinson's proposed list of pensioners (dated September 18, 1789), *ibid*, 766.

[26]Shaler, *Kentucky*, 137, 139, gives a concise treatment of the trials.

[27]Wilkinson listed Harry Innes ("attorney-general and counselor at law; gets 500 dollars a year from the state of Virginia"), Benjamin Sebastian ("lawyer from Virginia"), John Brown ("member of Congress"), Caleb Wallace ("one of our judges; enjoys a thousand dollars a year from the state of Virginia"), and John Fowler ("a man of influence"), with the comment, "These are my confidential friends and support my plan." He added the newly arrived General Lawsen to his list. In addition he named several prominent men under the titles, "These favor separation from the United States and a friendly connection with Spain," and, "These favor separation from Virginia but do not carry their views any further." *American Historical Review*, IX, 765.

[28]This is an elaborate document dated August 22, 1787. A translation appears in *ibid.*, IX, 496-491.

[29]The hatred of Great Britain and the enthusiasm for republican France shown in the Genêt incident of 1793 go far to confirm a negative answer. For Genêt's activities in Kentucky see McElroy, *Kentucky in the Nation's History*, 168, 186. The suspicion that the British in Canada encouraged the Indians in hostilities against the American frontier settlements naturally created much hard feeling. See for example, McElroy, *op. cit.*, 177. The antifederalist agitation in Kentucky in 1798 and 1799 should be kept in mind in connection with the general subject under discussion. This movement would suggest that the Kentuckians would

cated story which directly concern a study of monarchical tendencies in the United States. These questions have not been and perhaps never can be answered with absolute conviction. They may, however, be made more intelligible by the reflection that similar ones may be asked about other leaders and other frontier regions of the United States.

Acceptance of the protection of Great Britain was an alternative with the western settlers,[30] and that power had made overtures to the Americans,[31] according to General Wilkinson writing in September, 1789. The British officials, for their part, had reason to believe that there existed in the United States certain monarchical preferences. The "Opinions and Observations of Different Persons Respecting the United States," a secret service report, forwarded to Lord Sydney by the Governor of Canada in October, 1788,[32] contained several items of this nature. For instance, "some of the ablest members of the convention" had supported Hamilton's plan which "had in view the establishment of a monarchy, and the placing the crown upon the head of a foreign prince."[33] Again, "The ablest men in the States are at this moment strongly prepossessed in favor of our form of government, and they view the constitution which they are straining every nerve to establish, rather as an experiment, paving the way for a more energetic one, than as a final settlement of the country. . . ."[34]

As to Loyalists it was remarked that while "some of the most enlightened" had become Federalists, "from the persuasion that the re-union of the empire is impracticable," others were opposing the new constitution in the hope that the resultant distress might "produce what they have never lost sight of" [obviously reunion

never have submitted to monarchical rule. On the "Kentucky Resolutions" see McElroy, *op. cit.*, 211-264.

[30]*American Historical Review*, IX, 752. Compare 766.

[31]In his second memorial to Spain (September, 1789), Wilkinson declared he had rejected "honors and rewards offered . . . by Great Britain," and referred to flattering offers made to him "by Lord Dorchester through the medium of Colonel Conolly." *Ibid.*, IX, 758.

[32]*Report on Canadian Archives, 1890*, 100-106.

[33]*Ibid.*, 101.

[34]*Ibid.*, 101. Compare *ibid.*, 102, "Amongst the number of objections to the new system raised by the advocates for a monarchy, ..."

with Great Britain or the establishment of a government similar to that of the mother country].[35]

Several years later the lieutenant governor of Canada made some remarks and recommendations[36] which, taken apart from their context and away from their background, would be quite incomprehensible. "Should Congress adopt a Prince of the House of Brunswick for their future President or King, the happiness of the two nations would be interwoven and united—all jealousies removed & the most durable affections cemented that perhaps ever were formed between two Independent Nations."

"This is an object worthy the attention of Great Britain and which many of the most temperate men of the United States have in contemplation. And which many events, if once systematically begun, may hasten & bring to maturity."[37]

A study of the context suggests several significant facts. In the first place, the writer was much disturbed by the uncompromising spirit of the United States respecting the holding of the posts along the international boundary, the carrying on of trade and the wielding of influence among the Indians in the regions just south of the line.[38] In the second place, he was convinced that "until Messrs. Washington, Jefferson and Hamilton [should] have lost the direction of the . . . Confederation" no amicable settlement of these disputes, wholly fair to Great Britain, could be achieved. He declared that the overthrow of these administrators would be "less difficult to effect, by aiming at once to dissolve the Confederacy, than by any other secondary or indirect means."[39] In the third place, he credited the "general mass" of people of the United States with a "by no means defective" morality and good sense.[40] Finally, he urged that some "appeal to popular Reasoning must be made."[41] Simcoe's apparent hope

[35]On the other hand a "large and respectable proportion" took "little or no part in the general politics of the day," but began, "notwithstanding to rise in the estimation of the country," and were "courted," by both federalists and anti-federalists. *Report on Canadian Archives, 1890*, 102.

[36]"Lieutenant Governor J. G. Simcoe, Respecting Indians and Posts. Navy Hall, Niagara August 20th, 1792." *Michigan Pioneer and Historical Collections*, XXIV, 459-466.

[37]*Ibid.*, 466.

[38]*Ibid.*, 460-461.

[39]*Ibid.*, 460.

[40]*Ibid.*, 465.

[41]*Ibid.*, 466.

for a favorable outcome of such an appeal serves as something of a commentary on the convincing force of the reports on the existence of pro-British sentiment in the States.

The situation in "Kentucké and . . . Major General St. Clair's Government beyond the Ohio" was not overlooked in the "Opinions and Observations" of 1788. Doubt was expressed whether the new Congress would improve upon the old in respect to the assertion of authority over these frontier communities. The British observer referred to a report that some five hundred men, chiefly "officers and soldiers who served in the late continental army," were about to plant a colony west of the Mississippi.[42] They were "indifferent whether this measure may be agreeable to congress," they neither feared nor respected the Spaniards, and they were "desirious to open a friendly intercourse with our [the Canadian] government by the northern lakes" where they wished to carry on trade. All in all, "There [was] a general growing British interest in the states. . . ."[43]

A few months later, in the spring of 1789, Lord Dorchester was able to forward to Lord Sydney the "Desultory Reflexions By a Gentleman of Kentucky,"[44] which contained the following passage: "The politics of the western Country are verging fast to a crisis, and must speedily eventuate in an appeal to the patronage of Spain or Britain. No interruption can be apprehended from Congress, the seditious temper and jarring interests of the Atlantic States forbid general arrangements for the public good, and must involve a degree of imbecility, distraction and capricious policy, which a high toned monarchy can alone remedy;" but "the revolutions and changes necessary to reconcile the people to such a government, must involve much delay. Great Britain ought to prepare for the occasion, and she should employ the interval in forming confidential connexions, with men of enterprise, capacity, and popular influence, resident on western waters."[45] The mind of the Canadian governor and his correspondent in the home government must have been somewhat prepared for such a proposi-

[42]I. e., "upon the junction of the Mississippi and Missouri rivers on the northern bank."

[43]*Report on Canadian Archives, 1890*, 103.

[44]The author is identified as General Wilkinson by T. M. Green in his book, *The Spanish Conspiracy*, 297-298.

[45]*Report on Canadian Archives, 1890*, 107-108.

tion by the observation, included in the list of reports for the preceding year, that "a republican government does not seem calculated for the genius and disposition of the people in the states."[46]

The "Muskingum Settlements"[47] were reported[48] in 1790 to be "composed of disconnected" [sic][49] Continental Soldiers and officers who were attached to the United States by no other tye but personal regard for the President,[50] considering themselves as sacrificed by Congress and defrauded even in the sale of the lands they occupy."[51] This situation was suggested as the cause of their "extreme tenderness towards the British Government" in certain matters then at issue.[52] The "principal Body of People of Kentuckee" were "Friends of Great Britain," according to Lieutenant Governor Simcoe writing in 1791.[53]

A forceful denial of the probability of the triumph of separatism, stated by a competent observer who admitted such an event to be a possibility, is found in a letter from "General Rufus Putnam to Mr. Fisher Ames,"[54] of Massachusetts. The Ohio Company promoters, in seeking congressional grants in their behalf, had originally made much of the devotion to the federal union which, they said, characterized the would-be settlers of the northwest.[55] It is significant that Putnam, in attempting to prove the

[46]*Report on Canadian Archives, 1890*, 103.

[47]I. e., Marietta and neighboring regions.

[48]In an "Extract from a Private Letter from Detroit," signed "D," and indorsed "In Lord Dorchester to Mr. Grenville No. 74 of the 10th Novr. 1790."

[49]Discontented?

[50]One important reason for this regard was undoubtedly Washington's attitude towards the Ohio Company, an attitude of interest and encouragement. See W. P. and J. P. Cutler, *Life of Manasseh Cutler*, I, 144, 172-174.

[51]This statement is introduced with the words "It can do no harm to say that the Muskingum Settlements. . . ."

[52]I. e., in regard to a professed belief that British traders and not British officials were the source of the military supplies to Indians hostile to the United States. *Michigan Pioneer and Historical Collections*, XXIV, 105.

[53]Lieutenant Governor Simcoe to Henry Dundas, August 26, 1791. The reason cited was the difficulty of trading to the southward, even after Spanish concessions, because of the hostility of the Indians in that quarter. *Ibid.*, XXIV, 325.

[54]This letter was written on or before December 20, 1789, as Putnam refers to it in a letter of that date. He refrained from sending it to Ames until it should have been inspected by Cutler. Cutler, *op. cit.*, I, 450, and II, 373-383.

[55]*Ibid.*, I, 121, 134, 147, and especially 304.

improbability of separatism, does not mention this devotion but instead rests his argument on the assertion "that it is and always will be the interest of the Western country to remain a part of the United States."[56] With a few simple but impressive arguments he shows that the Canadian government "can never suit [the] genius, nor be for [the] interest" of the westerners, and that "the advantage to be derived from the Spanish Government" is not "much better."[57] He does, however, issue the following warning: "I do not deny but what such circumstances may exist as shall not only make it the wish of some, but of all, the inhabitants of that country to be separated from the old States, . . should Congress give up her claim to the navigation of the Mississippi or cede it to the Spaniards, I believe the people in the Western quarter would separate themselves from the United States very soon. Such measure, I have no doubt, would excite so much rage and dissatisfaction that the people would sooner put themselves under the despotic government of Spain than remain the indented servants of Congress; or should Congress by any means fail to give the inhabitants . . . such protection as their present infant state requires . . . ; in that case such events may take place as will oblige the inhabitants of that country to put themselves under the protection of Great Britain or Spain."[58] He also professes to believe that ambitious men, more interested in "the emoluments of office than the public good" are in this region as everywhere and "may influence people to pursue, as the object of their happiness, measures which will end in their ruin."[59]

Before accepting these assertions at their face value the circumstances under which they were made must be called to mind. In the first place, no man held the success of the Ohio Company more dear than did Rufus Putnam.[60] In the second place, the assertions were made at a time when the project was handicapped by the delay in closing the land grant deal with Congress,[61] the inadequacy of military protection against the Indians,[62] and, in

[56]Cutler, *op. cit.*, II, 377.

[57]*Ibid.*, II, 375.

[58]*Ibid.*, II, 377.

[59]*Ibid.*, II, 377.

[60]His interest may be traced, in good part, by following the references to him in the index to *ibid.*, II, 488.

[61]See *ibid.*, I, 445, 447, 449, 450.

[62]See, for example, *ibid.*, I, 447-448.

common with their more southern neighbors, uncertainty as to the opening of the Mississippi to their trade.[63] Finally, the assertions were made in a letter, known to have been an object of special care to its author, and addressed to one of the most influential statesmen of a district reputed with some reason to entertain a degree of hostility towards the development of the West. Under such circumstances Putnam could hardly be expected entirely to discredit reports of such strategic worth in a struggle for measures favorable to the western frontier settlements. On the other hand, Washington himself, a few years earlier, had written, "The western states (I speak now from my own observation) stand, as it were, upon a pivot. The touch of a feather would turn them either way."[64]

It has been pointed out that certain leaders of the Ohio Company such as Tupper and Varnum, could conceive of the establishment of a monarchical government in the United States.[65] Nicola, whose monarchical propositions to Washington have been discussed in an earlier chapter, associated with these propositions a plan for a military colony in the West,[66] not unlike that of Pickering's which was a forerunner of the Ohio Company.[67] The present writer has been unable to establish any definite relationship between Nathaniel Gorham, suspected monarchist, and the Ohio group, but like them he was interested in vast land projects along the frontier.[68] He quite obviously believed that separation would prevail in the West for in the Convention he said, "It is not to be supposed that the Govt will last long enough" to make the numbers of representatives excessive, for "Can it be supposed that this vast Country including the Western territory will 150 years hence remain one nation?"[69] Through his activities in state and national politics he must have come into close contact with some of the group. The evidence suggests that some general identity of interest appears among persons supposed to have con-

[63]Cutler, *op. cit.*, II, 374.

[64]Washington to Governor Harrison of Virginia, October, 1784, *ibid.*, II, 388.

[65]See above, pages 73 and 47.

[66]See above, page 44.

[67]For Pickering's plan, see Cutler, *op. cit.*, I, 156-159.

[68]See above, page 67.

[69]Quoted above, page 69.

sidered monarchical institutions feasible for the United States.[70] Incidentally, the possibilities of such a suggestion are tremendous for it points to the probability that many other like-minded persons were not averse to such institutions even though the occasion did not arise for an expression of their opinions on the subject.

Other evidence is not lacking to indicate that separatism was a well recognized tendency at the time.[71] The evidence suggesting that this spirit, in the West, involved a tolerance of monarchical institutions as a means to an end, though not as an end in themselves, speaks for itself. One further episode deserves attention in this connection, namely, the final negotiations between the Vermont separatists and Great Britain.

Vermont, by virtue of her unique position of practical independence,[72] was able to negotiate with the British in a more nearly official manner than could the other districts. Her motives for conducting such negotiations were similar to those of the West, namely, a desire for a convenient and unobstructed channel for her trade, and a distrust of Congress as a champion of her interests. It has been said that "a strong party in the Sovereign State of Vermont was against joining the Union, and favored an alliance with Great Britain, or even return to British rule."[73]

No year since the peace of 1783 had passed without negotiations between Vermonters and British officials.[74] The majority concerned petitions for a commercial treaty or other commercial concessions but some went much farther. Thus certain leaders of the Green Mountain State had, at the close of the War, declared themselves in favor of annexation by Canada.

[70]See above, page 74.

[71]Washington had proceeded to urge the construction of thoroughfares for trade between coast and interior regions. In this connection it should be remembered that Washington was financially interested in western land projects.

[72]On this position see "Vermont as a Sovereign and Independent State, 1783 to 1791," *Vermont Historical Society Collections*, II, 395-498, as well as the treatment of this period in any history of the state.

[73]*The American Historical Review*, XXI, 547-560, prints an article on this theme by S. F. Bemis, under the title "Relations between the Vermont Separatists and Great Britain, 1789-1791." The documents upon which the article is based are described as a selection from "The Colonial Office Papers in the British Public Record Office" transcripts of most of which "are in the Canadian Archives at Ottawa, series Q." The author of the article consulted documents in both of these repositories. *Ibid.*, 548.

[74]Compare *ibid.*, XXI, 548-550.

Ethan Allen, writing in 1788 a memorial full of defiance towards the United States, told Lord Dorchester that "the leading men in Vermont [were] not sentimentally attached to a republican form of government."[75] They were, however, "determined to maintain their present mode of it, till they [could] have a better, and expect to be able to do it, at least, so long as the United States will be able to maintain theirs, or until they can on principles of mutual interest and advantage return to the British government, without war or annoyance from the United States."[76]

Despite these protestations of attachment, the Vermonters did not receive the concessions which Ethan Allen sought.[77] Hence another of the Allen brothers journeyed to England in the interest of the petition. In introducing Levi Allen[78] a curious and perhaps significant coincidence between his circumstances and those of James Wilkinson is worth noting. Wilkinson in his dealings with Spain had made much of the contention that concessions enabling him, individually, to convey goods through Spanish territory[79] and to sell them at low prices to the Kentuckians would be a powerful agent in developing a pro-Spanish political senti-

[75]Allen to Lord Dorchester, July 16, 1788. Quoted in *American Historical Review*, XXI, 550. Calendared with "liberal quotations," in *Report on Canadian Archives, 1890*, State Papers, 210-211.

Bemis calls attention to the interesting fact that "this was presented to the governor of Canada within a few months from the time when Wilkinson forwarded a similar communication to the Spanish governor at New Orleans." *American Historical Review*, XXI, 550.

[76]Allen goes so far as to say that "should the United States attempt a conquest of them" [the Vermonters], he presumes they would yield their independence and "become a province of Great Britain" just as they would "readily" have done so in "the time of General Haldimand's command, could Great Britain have afforded Vermont protection." *Report on Canadian Archives*, *1890*, 211.

[77]Several important concessions were, however, made from time to time. (See Bemis, article cited, *American Historical Review*, XXI, 549, also letter from Simcoe to Dundas, August 2, 1791, *Report on Canadian Archives*, *1889*, 53.) But a commercial treaty, as desired by the Vermont petitioners, was declared impossible.

[78]Levi Allen received a pension as a loyalist according to Lieutenant Governor Simcoe; *Report on Canadian Archives*, *1889*, 53. For activities of a third brother, Ira, see above, page 36. For an example of the united efforts of the Allens see *ibid.*, 1890, 210, (letter of July 16, 1788). Compare "The Allen brothers, Ethan, Ira, and Levi, were the most active and versatile of the separatist party. . . ." Bemis, *op. cit.*, *American Historical Review*, XXI, 548.

[79]New Orleans and vicinity.

ment in that region.[80] Similarly Allen contended for such concessions as would enable him to bring English goods through Canada for sale at attractive prices in Vermont.[81] Whether Allen and Wilkinson were really seeking to effect political arrangements for the general welfare, or whether their declared object was merely a cloak for their personal ambitions is a legitimate but probably unanswerable question. Whatever the answer Allen's methods acquire added interest when compared with those of the Kentuckian. On the whole the former's assertions were the bolder and more sweeping of the two. Thus Allen solemnly assured a British secretary of state that during the Revolutionary War "at least three fourths" of the inhabitants of Vermont were loyal to the mother country and that "those of the Inhabitants, who in the beginning of the frenzy . . even for a time opposed to His Majesty's Government, soon saw their error and would have been happy to have . . . returned to their Allegiance long before the end of the war. . . ."[82] They were, according to Allen, still desirous of making this move but for "doubt with respect to its practicability." The fact that the writer claimed, even though without good reason,[83] to be "authorized by Commission under the Great Seal of Vermont, pursuant to an Act of the General Assembly thereof, to negotiate a commercial and Friendly Intercourse between Vermont and his Majesty's Dominions" must have given his words some weight.[84]

In one of his last communications on the subject, Levi Allen declared to Henry Dundas, home secretary at the time, that the "Principal men of Governor Chittenden and Allen's Party"

[80] *American Historical Review*, IX, 763.

[81] See especially the letter from Levi Allen to Lieutenant Governor Simcoe, November 19, 1791, *Report on Canadian Archives, 1889*, 56. A very similar letter, dated November 27, 1791, is printed in the *American Historical Review*, XXI, 559-560.

[82] Memorial of Levi Allen, May 4, 1789, *American Historical Review*, XXI, 553. Allen even declared that due to Vermont's natural and advantageous commercial connection with Canada (dependent in turn on the "locality of Vermont, as well as the Disposition of its Inhabitants") the Vermonters had "earnestly hoped to have been incorporated as an appendage to the Province of Quebec, but those hopes were defeated by the boundary line of the United States as settled by the late Peace." *Ibid.*, 553-554.

[83] This point is treated in a footnote, *ibid.*, XXI, 553.

[84] See Lieutenant Governor Simcoe's reference to this commission, *Report on Canadian Archives, 1889*, 53.

had told him "to assure the British Court that Vermont was from local situation as well as from inclination firmly attached to them, and that whenever Vermont should find it necessary to join Britain or join Congress, they would positively join the former."[85]

For some time, until the British government had made sure that the United States would not break the peace in order to secure Detroit and the other border posts, that government, involved in the Nootka Sound controversy, found it worth its while to attempt to develop sentiment favorable to itself in Vermont, as also in Kentucky.[86] The governor of Upper Canada, indeed, continued to urge the extreme strategic importance of these states for some years longer.[87] But Vermont's acceptance of admittance into the Union, in 1791,[88] forced Levi Allen to admit the futility of further negotiations between his state and Great Britain.[89] Lieutenant Governor Simcoe's optimism could overlook even this event and forsee the development under proper tutelage, of a British interest in Vermont and Kentucky, as opposed to the rest of the Union.[90] Still later Simcoe reported that all of the people of Vermont[91] with whom he had spoken agreed that Vermont would "support a neutrality" in case of war between the United States and Great Britain.[92] A statement, apparently of the same period, preserved

[85]*American Historical Review*, XXI, 555. Similar declarations were made by Vermonters in 1794 according to Simcoe and Jarvis. *Report on Canadian Archives, 1889*, 57, 58.

[86]Concisely treated, with footnote references, in the article by Bemis, *American Historical Review*, XXI, 551. Simcoe was especially solicitous about this matter as appears in his letter to Mr. Dundas, August 2, 1791. *Report on Canadian Archives, 1889*, 54-55.

[87]See Simcoe's letter to Mr. Dundas, August 5, 1794, *ibid.*, 57-58.

[88]For expressions of Levi Allen's opposition to such action by Vermont see his letters to Dundas, August 9th and November 27th, 1791, *American Historical Review*, XXI, 557 and 560 respectively. The letter of November 27th contains a curious passage in which Allen ascribes Vermont's regrettable mistake in this respect to the death, absence, or defection of her leaders. *Ibid.*, 560, but more forcefully given in *Report on Canadian Archives, 1889*, 56.

[89]*American Historical Review*, XXI, 560.

[90]*Report on Canadian Archives, 1889*, 54-55.

[91]He had described them earlier in his letter as "some very respectable people of Vermont." *Ibid.*, 57.

[92]*Ibid.*, 57.

in the Canadian Archives,[93] quotes Governor Chittenden as saying "that if Congress takes a part in the War in favor of France I am sure Vermont will never accede to it but will make the best bargain they can for themselves . . ." The Vermont executive was further quoted as follows; " . . . glve [give] my compliments to Governor Simcoe, and tell him that the Governor and Council of Vermont are of the same opinion that they were in the year 1781 when Colonel Fay was . . . negotiating a union with Canada &c. &c. when the news of Lord Cornwallis's misfortune reached Vermont, which suspended the negotiation and finally put an end to it. That Vermont has nothing to gain by entering into a combination to defend the Sea Coasts, on the contrary everything to lose—their Commerce (through Canada) ruined, their whole Country open to inroads of British Indians, &c."[94]

The Vermont episode may be said to close the story of separatist movements in relation to monarchical tendencies. The Blount Conspiracy, so-called, of the middle nineties, although involving a military alliance between the western frontiersmen and the British[95] (against the Spanish possessions in the southwest), did not go to the length of political union as suggested in the Vermont and Kentucky negotiations.

The leading features of these embryonic separatist movements[96] can be stated quite definitely despite the seeming impossibility of handing down a final decision on the motives and intentions which actuated them. These features may be summarized as follows: First and foremost, the avowed ascendancy of economic interests over political preferences; second, a professed willingness for close association and even allegiance to a monarchical government to effect the aforesaid economic ends; third, the absence of any desire to *create* monarchical institutions either for

[93]This is preserved in the same volume (Archives, series Q, vol. 281-1), and on a page close to Simcoe's letter to Dundas of August 5, 1794, entitled "Statement by Mr. Jarvis," and signed with Simcoe's initials, "J. G. S." *Report on Canadian Archives, 1889*, 58.

[94]*Ibid.*, 58.

[95]See concise statement by F. J. Turner in the *American Historical Review*, X, 273-275, also 574-606.

[96]This summary applies to the Vermont negotiations of 1780-1783, discussed above, pages 35 to 39, as well as to the various episodes considered in the pages immediately preceding the summary.

particular areas or for the United States as a whole; fourth, the restriction of the expression of what may be called monarchical leanings to a few "leading men" and the absence of any such expression on the part of the people as a whole.

No definite projects for the erection of a monarchy by the Federalists during the twelve years of their control have ever been discovered. A special student of New England federalism (Dr. Samuel Eliot Morison), writes, "I have never seen any evidence of a conscious trend to monarchy on the part of the Federalists even in their private correspondence, after 1789. . . . After the ratification of the Constitution the Federalists devoted their energies to strengthening and energizing republican government. They realized that a monarchy in the United States would be an absurdity, and that the best chance of preserving the institutions that they believed in was to support the Federal and the State governments."[97] Yet these were the very years in which most of the "monarchical" accusations were made. The author of the "Life of John Marshall" has noted that in gathering and adjusting material for that work he was "profoundly impressed by what seemed to be the honest belief of many apparently sensible men that there was a monarchical movement" on foot. Again he says, "Undoubtedly there was a general fear that certain men were plotting to establish a monarchy or at least that they preferred a monarchy to a republic, but this fear had been planted by politicians, sincere and insincere, in the minds of the people, the masses of whom at that time were singularly uninformed, suspicious and isolated."[98]

There seems to have been general agreement in 1789 that Washington had no thought of personal aggrandizement in accepting the presidential chair. When the organizers of the new government showed some inclination to make it a presidential throne[99] the opponents of royal trappings found in Vice President

[97]In reply to questions by the present writer, Dr. Morison also writes, "I admit that there was more or less loose talk in high Federalist society about the superiority of a monarchy over a republic and the likelihood that the logic of events would lead to monarchy, if not to military despotism. But this same sort of talk has been going on in society to this day." Compare footnote 100 above, page 98.

[98]Mr. Albert J. Beveridge in a letter to the writer.

[99]See account of Senate discussion, May 7, 1789, W. Maclay, *Journal* (E. S. Maclay ed.), 21. On titles see Madison, *Writings* (Hunt ed.), V, 369-370 n.; *Massachusetts Historical Society Collections*, 5th ser., IV, 436–439; 6th. ser., IV, 432;

Adams a closer target for reproach than the President.[100] As for the ceremony with which Washington surrounded himself, it was probably excused by most of the persons who would otherwise have opposed it, on the grounds that Washington's motives were pure and his situation novel and puzzling.[101] A member of the first Senate remarked of Washington, in May, 1789, that "Whether he will be able to retain his usual popularity, time must determine, but I am very much mistaken if he ever justly forfeits it."[102]

By 1793 attacks upon Washington by the opposition press were becoming articulate. These attacks were closely connected with ultra-democratic enthusiasm for the French Revolution, and especially for the antimonarchical stage it had attained by the time of the execution of the King. "Hundreds of examples might be given showing the same supersensitive, silly, trivial, maudlin state of mind prevailing among a large section of the American public as prevailed in France, and which was derived largely from France. . . . Evidences of royalty were attacked. A medallion of George III on a Philadelphia church was ordered removed by the Democrats, because to their knowledge it had a tendency to keep young and virtuous men from attending public worship."[103] On the other hand, a good deal of respect is due to the obvious sincerity of many Americans who believed that a failure to assist the French revolutionists was nothing short of flagrant ingratitude in view of French aid to the American revoltionary cause. Washington's proclamation of neutrality, or rather, discontent with it, formed a rallying point for the opposition party which was gradually forming in the United States. Its members were in no mood to be reminded that the royal government of France had been the source of French aid to the Americans and the signatory of the treaty of alliance. They went so far as to accuse their President

Massachusetts Historical Society Proceedings, 2d ser., XV, 129, 132; *Wisconsin Historical Publications*, LXIII, 97.

[100]See for example, Maclay, *op. cit.*, 10-14. These pages afford an excellent illustration of the significance attached to monarchical formulae.

[101]*Ibid.*, 15.

[102]Paine Wingate, of New Hampshire, in a letter to Jeremy Belknap, May 12, 1789. *Massachusetts Historical Society Collections*, 6th ser., IV, 432.

[103]These lines are quoted from a vivid, though perhaps too unsympathetic, portrayal of the situation in C. D. Hazen's article "The French Revolution as Seen by the Americans of the Eighteenth Century" in *American Historical Association Report, 1895*, 455-466.

of cherishing kingly ambitions in keeping with his anti-republican stand on the French situation. These accusations were so persistent and irritating that Washington is said finally to have exclaimed "that he had rather be on his farm than to be made *emperor of the world* and yet that they were charging him with wanting to be a king."[104] The imprudent behavior of the minister Genêt, in appealing from the President to the people, however, influenced many "French enthusiasts" to once more support President Washington.[105]

The administration's show of force against the so-called "Whiskey Insurrection" in western Pennsylvania, in the fall of 1794, renewed hostility to the President. As the Federalists expressed it "every measure of THE PRESIDENT'S" had been declared "the most abominable stretch of power."[106] What especially turned the opposition party against Washington was his signing of the Jay treaty with England,[107] a treaty, according to the "Aurora," which would have annihilated "every republican principle in the government, had not the . . . spirited exertions of our patriotic representatives" prevented.[108] Adet reported to the French Committee of Public Safety that Washington was ruled not by patriotism but ambition, and associated the President with monarchism.[109] The "Spurious Letters" of Washington published as though authentic, were used at the time of the treaty agitation, to convince the public that Washington, even in the Revolution, had cherished the British monarchical government.[110] The "Aurora," early in 1797, printed an article by "A

[104]"The Anas," Jefferson, *Writings* (Ford ed.), I, 254.

[105]Compare Bassett, *Short History of the United States*, 266-267.

[106]*Gazette of the United States*, Sept. 6, 1794, quoting from the *Columbian Centinel.*

[107]For evidences of deep interest in European affairs see, for example, *American Historical Association Report*, 1896, I, 795-796; Jay, *Correspondence*, IV, 198-203. See also above, n. 22.

[108]*Aurora*, Sept. 29, 1797, p. 2. Compare J. Jones to Madison, early in 1795, *Massachusetts Historical Society Proceedings*, 2d. ser., XV, 147; also letters by Jones, Dec. 21, 1795, Feb. 17 and Apr. 26, 1796, *ibid.*, 153, 155, 156; letters by Henry Tazewell, Jan. 24, Apr. 4, and Dec. 18, 1796, Tazewell, *Twelve Letters*, Manuscripts Division, Library of Congress.

[109]Sept. 2, 1795, *American Historical Association Report, 1903*, II, 776-777. See also letter from Adet to the French Minister of Foreign Relations, *ibid.*, 915-916.

[110]W. C. Ford, *Spurious Letters of Washington.*

native of Pennsylvania" who said, "I should have expected that we had not so soon arrived at the threshold of monarchy, that any one would assert that the Chief Magistrate is not amenable to the people for his conduct." The article justified an "appeal to the people" which the French representative Adet had just made public.[111] The issues of this paper, throughout the month, fairly bristled with insinuations of Washington's monarchism.[112] Even after Washington's retirement to private life the French Consul General reported that the Federalists wished to make Washington king.[113]

During the first part of the administration of his successor Washington was exempt from monarchical charges. The "Aurora" even praised him, indirectly, for having refused "the diadem offered by his veteran army."[114] But Washington's appointment as head of the army raised against France in 1798 once more brought him into ill repute with the opposition party. In the campaign literature of 1800 Washington was dubbed the "monarch of Mount-Vernon,"[115] and denounced for encouraging in America an imitation of royal birthday celebrations, royal levees, and royal speeches from the throne.[116]

The final verdict by the opposition party as to the monarchism of Washington can be best expressed in Jefferson's words, "I am convinced he is more deeply seated in the love and gratitude of the republicans, than in the Pharisaical homage of the federal

[111]Jan. 5, 1797, p. 2.

[112]Satirizing the praise accorded him for his revolutionary services, denouncing his support of "hereditary succession" in upholding a definite candidate for the next administration, challenging him to deny that he held the views set forth in the "Letters", charging him (indirectly) with having exploited his popularity, and scoffing at his "Farewell Address." See issues for Jan. 6, p. 2; Jan. 7, p. 2; Jan. 9, p. 3; Jan. 23, p. 3; Jan. 26, p. 3.

[113]After mentioning the agreement of England and the Federalists that the United States should declare war on France, Adet remarks, "Le but de toutes leurs menées est d'avoir un roi, mais l'un voudroit que ce fût un des fils du roi d'Angleterre, et l'autre Washington." Létombe to French Minister of Foreign Relations, June 18, 1797, *American Historical Association Report, 1903,* II, 1038.

[114]There is nothing to show that the Nicola propositions were known, as a knowledge of the "Newburgh Address" would sufficiently account for the above reference. See *Aurora,* Jan. 29, 1800, p. 2.

[115]J. T. Callender, *Prospect before us,* 18.

[116]T. Coxe, *Strictures upon the letter imputed to Mr. Jefferson, addressed to Mr. Mazzei,* 4-5.

monarchists. For he was no monarchist from preference of his judgment. . . . He has often declared to me that he considered our new constitution as an experiment on the practicability of republican government . . . that he was determined the experiment should have a fair trial, and would lose the last drop of his blood in support of it."[117]

Monarchical charges were brought with less restraint and more reason against Washington's successor as President; with less restraint because Adams did not enjoy the nation wide popularity of the military hero,[118] and with more reason because of certain of his own actions and utterances. Despite his early reputation as an ardent republican[119] even before the adoption of the Constitution Adams had been suspected of monarchical preferences, due to his "Defence of the American Constitutions."[120] Adams had "thrown together some hasty speculations upon . . government" under the stress of his alarm over "the commotions in New England" at the time of the Shays Rebellion.[121] There were those who suspected that "under ye mask of attacking Mr. Turgot" who had criticized the American form of government, Mr. Adams "notwithstanding now and then a saving clause" was "insidiously attempting . . . to overturn" the American constitutions.[122] In Washington's administration Adams had been satirized as "The Dangerous Vice."[123] His advocacy of ceremonial in the new government was mercilessly ridiculed by some as of a monarchical character.[124] In his advice to Washington on the matter, in May, 1789, Adams declared that the presidency "by its legal authority, defined in the constitution, has no equal in the world, excepting those only which are

[117]Letter of Jan. 2, 1814, Jefferson, *Writings* (Ford ed.), IX, 449-450.

[118]Compare Adet to the French Minister of Foreign Relations, Dec. 15, 1796, *American Historical Association Report*, 1903, II, 978-979.

[119]See above, pages 23, and 34.

[120]See above, p. 87.

[121]See his own statement in a letter of Jan. 27, 1797, *Works*, IX, 551.

[122]The Reverend James Madison to his son, June 11, 1787, *Massachusetts Historical Society Proceedings*, 2d ser., XVII, 465, 467. Compare letters between W. Nelson and W. Short, July 7 and Sept. 17, 1787; March 9, 13, 1788, *Short Papers*, Manuscripts Division, Library of Congress.

[123]See *Massachusetts Historical Society Proceedings*, XI, 18, for an example of such a reference.

[124]Maclay, *Journal*, 10-14, 155, is probably the best example.

held by crowned heads; nor is the royal authority in all cases to be compared to it."[125] In a series of letters to Roger Sherman, in July, 1789, Adams proved, to his own satisfaction, that the United States was actually a "monarchical republic, or . . . a limited monarchy."[126] Yet in 1790 he was cautioning a correspondent against the "fraudulent use of the words *monarchy* and *republic*," and declaring himself "a mortal and irreconcilable enemy to monarchy."[127] His opposition to the French Revolution especially as expressed in his "Discourses on Davila" was "urged as . . . proof, that he was an advocate for monarchy, and laboring to introduce a hereditary president in America."[128] After the outbreak of the war between England and France Adam's eulogies of the British constitution were more distasteful than ever to those of his political opponents who "admired everything French and hated everything English." By 1796, M. Adet was reporting that the "Senators and John Adams at their head," were declaring that a monarchy was the only government suitable to any people.[129] At almost the same time Jefferson wrote his much discussed "Letter to Mazzei" in which he said that "an Anglican monarchical, & aristocratical party has sprung up whose avowed object is to draw over us the substance, as they have already done the forms, of the British government. The main body of our citizens . . . remain true to their republican principles . . . Against us are the Executive, the Judiciary, two out of three branches of the legislature . . ."[130] After the election of Adams, but before his inauguration, the issue was again discussed. Representative Robert G. Harper quoted from the "Defence" itself to prove Adams was no monarchist.[131] In op-

[125] Adams, *Works*, VIII, 493.

[126] *Ibid.*, VI, 430.

[127] Letter to Benjamin Rush, Apr. 18, 1790, Adams, *Works*, IX, 566. Compare letter to Jefferson, July 29, 1791, *ibid.*, VIII, 507.

[128] See "Discourses on Davila," *ibid.*, VI, 225-403. Note also letters of 1792, in Madison, *Writings* (Hunt ed.), VI, 50, n., and *Massachusetts Historical Society Proceedings*, 2d ser., XV, 140.

[129] In the original French, this reads, ". . . le seul Gouvernement convenable, à tous les Peuples." Adet to the Minister of Foreign Relations, May 3, 1796, *American Historical Association Report*, 1903, II, 901. Compare letters of Sept. 24 and Dec. 15, 1796, *ibid.*, 949, 979.

[130] Jefferson to P. Mazzei, April 24, 1796, *Writings* (Ford ed.), VII, 75-76.

[131] Letter to his constituents, Jan. 5, 1797, *American Historical Association Report, 1913*, II, 26.

position quarters the suggestion was made that once in office as president he would perhaps be guided by the constitution and not attempt to put his monarchical theories into effect.[132]

In his inaugural address Adams did not overlook suspicions of his monarchical preferences for he was careful to state his "preference upon principle of a free republican government, formed upon long and serious reflection, after a diligent and impartial inquiry after truth," and avowed "a conscientious determination" to support the Constitution "until it shall be altered by the judgments and the wishes of the people, expressed in the mode prescribed in it."[133] Nevertheless, the charges against him were continued throughout the year.[134]

Party feeling was at an especially high pitch in 1798 even before the passage of the alien, sedition, and other acts of defence. The "Aurora," February twenty-seventh of that year, said that the President's dictatorial attitude towards Congress in respect to war or peace with France was leading "not merely to monarchy, but despotism."[135] In March an article appeared proving the "Presidential supremacy over a King of England," urging that the President's powers of patronage exceeded those of the latter dignitary.[136] The "Aurora" had concluded by the end of the month that the "royal faction" was about to get its war with France unless the people should rouse themselves soon.[137] James Madison observed of the President's message that it was "only a further development to the public, of the violent passions, & heretical politics, which have been long privately known to govern him."[138] The disclosure by Adams of the X. Y. Z. correspondence did not unite all persons to the administration. Henry Tazewell declared that the proofs were "innumerable and incontrovertible" that the "great political object of our own Govt." had "from the beginning been to assimilate it to that of Great Britain." He named

[132]See the *Aurora*, Feb. 3, 1797, p. 3; J. Jones to Madison, Jan. 29 and Feb. 5, 1797, *Massachusetts Historical Society Proceedings*, 2d ser., XV, 159, 160.

[133]Adams, *Works*, IX, 109.

[134]See the *Aurora*, July 8, p. 2; July 14, p. 3; Aug. 14, p. 2; Sept. 27, p. 3; Sept. 29, p. 2; also *American Historical Association Report, 1903*, II, 1038, 1090. See Appendix B, I, 1, "Cobbett."

[135]*Aurora*, Feb. 27, 1798, p. 2.

[136]*Ibid.*, Mar. 5, 1798, p. 3.

[137]*Ibid.*, Mar. 30, 1798, p. 3.

[138]Madison, *Writings* (Hunt ed.), VI, 312. (Letter to Jefferson, Apr. 2, 1798.)

the "laws, and public acts of the Government" as the proofs he had in mind. He declared that "every measure of defence" against France was "made the means of increasing the power of the Executive."[139] Livingston's attack upon the Alien Bill as making the President a despot was published with the declaration that a code was being advocated "compared to which the ordeal is wise, & the trial by battle . . . merciful and just."[140] "Richard Frugal" wrote to Mr. Bache,[141] in July, "Immediately . . . on the passing of the alien bill— Egad says I, I have found use for the bastile key and . . . for . . . the bastile itself . . . and the famous Lettres de Cachet."[142] Other accounts attacked the President or deplored the "system of terror that has been countenanced by our administration."[143] The most formal protest was voiced in the Virginia Resolutions of 1798 which declared that the spirit "manifested by the federal government to enlarge its powers by forced constructions" of the Constitution would inevitably result in transforming "the present republican system of the United States into an absolute or, at best, a mixed monarchy."[144] In 1799 the "tyrannical and degrading effects"[145] of the Sedition Act were harped upon, monarchical developments were described as inevitable among any people,[146] and the ceremonious attendance of the President at the theatre deplored as meant "to familiarise us with the forms of monarchy."[147] The "Federalists" were defined as men who for the most part were beginning "to think a limited monarchy more tolerable than was heretofore supposed."[148] A satirical article, really amusing from its very thoroughness, described the procedure at a Federalist Independence Day celebration as including an "ingenious, learned, and eloquent harrangue upon the blessings of monarchical forms of governments, and the

[139]May 9, 1798, H. Tazewell, *Twelve Letters*. Manuscripts Division, Library of Congress.

[140]*Aurora*, July 2, 1798, p. 2.

[141]Editor of the *Aurora*.

[142]*Aurora*, July 3, 1798, p. 2.

[143]*Ibid.*, July 4, 1798, p. 2; and July 7, p. 3; July 12, p. 3; July 25, p. 2; Aug. 27, p. 2.

[144]Elliot, *Debates*, IV, 528.

[145]*Aurora*, Feb. 21, 1799, p. 3.

[146]*Ibid.*, Feb. 7, 1799, p. 2.

[147]*Ibid.*, Feb. 22, 1799; p. 3.

[148]*Ibid.*, July 4, 1799, p. 3.

advantages of standing armies." The toast to "The Day" was accompanied by "3 laughs—a groan," while that to "The King of England" was followed by "16 cheers, 16 guns and 9 bumpers round."[149] English immigrants were declared to secretly favor the placing of a British prince on a throne in the United States, by means of the British army and its allies, once they had reduced the regicides of France.[150]

Even the President's break with the extremists of his own party, by making peace with France, did not ward off monarchical charges in the presidential election of 1800. An account of his alleged declaration that he had long been contending against the monarchists included a statement that at the same time he had said "that we shall never have liberty or happiness in this country, until our first Magistrate is hereditary."[151] An absurd tale was circulated that Adams was to "unite his family with the Royal House of Great Britain, the bridegroom to be King of America."[152] A more reasonable attack was on the score of the praise of monarchy in his "Defence, or rather attack of the American constitutions."[153] The author of "The Political Science of John Adams" writes of our second President, "Even for America he was a determined advocate of the elective principle only in the case of the house of representatives. In the other two branches he admitted the coming necessity of the hereditary principle, and recommended its adoption when the proper time should arrive. Had he lived till the advent of that time, or had the time arrived during his life, he would have advocated its actual adoption. . . . It was, therefore, by no means an unjustifiable use of language for his opponents to class him as a monarchist." Adams himself left the question more in doubt when he remarked of an "hereditary nobility or Senate" that it was essential to an "*hereditary limited* monarchy" but was "unattainable and impracticable" in America, and added, "I should scarcely be for it, if it were."[154] On the

[149] *Aurora*, July 18, 1799, p. 2.

[150] *Ibid.*, Aug. 17, 1799, p. 3.

[151] "The Monarchism and the Foreign Devotion, of Persons in the Government of the Union, established on the testimony of Mr. Adams," *Aurora*, Sept. 26, 1800, p. 2.

[152] Cited by A. J. Beveridge, *Life of John Marshall*, I, 290-291.

[153] Callender, *Prospect Before Us*, 37.

[154] Letter to B. Rush, Apr. 18, 1790, Adams, *Works*, IX, 566.

other hand, Mr. Walsh believes Adams's adherence to the theory that the people were the "source of all government, stood him in good stead" with the people,[155] which seems very probable. Thomas Jefferson, in 1818, wrote a plausible and in many respects a satisfying interpretation of Adams. "Mr. Adams had originally been a republican. The glare of royalty and nobility, during his mission to England, had made him believe their fascination a necessary ingredient in government, and Shay's rebellion, not sufficiently understood where he then was, seemed to prove that the absence of want and oppression was not a sufficient guarantee of order. His book on the American constitutions having made known his political bias, he was taken up by the monarchical federalists, in his absence, and on his return to the U. S. he was by them made to believe that the general disposition of our citizens was favorable to monarchy . . . Mr. Adams, I am sure, has . . . since thoroughly seen that his constituents were devoted to republican government, and whether his judgment is re-settled . . . or not, his is conformed as a good citizen to the will of the majority, and would now, I am persuaded, maintain it's republican structure with the zeal and fidelity belonging to his character."[156]

A study of the Federalist administrations would not be complete without some reference to Alexander Hamilton. Recognized by Jefferson as the "Colossus" of the Federalist party, he seemed a dangerous man to the "republicans." Associated most especially with the unpopular financial measures of the early part of Washington's administration he was thought, by his funding schemes, to be sowing the "seeds of hereditary power."[157] There is every reason to accept Hamilton's own statement of his stand, as found in a letter to Edward Carrington, early in 1792. He declared his real attachment "to the republican theory" and had "strong hopes of the success of that theory." At the same time

[155]C. M. Walsh, *Political Science of John Adams,* 283-284. For Jefferson's analysis of the monarchism of Adams see Jefferson, *Writings* (Ford ed.), I, 166, and X, 332. For an explanation by Adams himself see letter to Benjamin Rush, April 18, 1790, Adams, *Works,* IX, 566.

[156]Preface to "The Anas," Jefferson, *Writings* (Ford ed.), I, 166-167. See above, pages 22-23, for references to Adams's views in 1776.

[157]Compare Benjamin Rush to Jeremy Belknap, June 21, 1792, in *Belknap Papers,* III (*Massachusetts Historical Society Collections,* 6th ser., IV), 527; also Jefferson, *Writings* (Ford ed.), I, 165.

he considered "its success as yet a problem." His whole political philosophy may be learned from the following sentence, "It is yet to be determined by experience whether it [republicanism] be consistent with that stability and order in government which are essential to public strength and private security and happiness."[158] His prominence in the suppression of the "Whiskey Insurrection" seemed to his opponents to prove him an advocate for "crushing down the spirit of republicanism by FORCE OF ARMS!"[159] M. Adet, in 1795, professed to believe that Hamilton had been currying favor with the British [by means of his advocacy of the Jay Treaty] in order to further his own advancement by some monarchical arrangement.[160] During Washington's administration Hamilton played the rôle of a king's minister of the old days, in being the target for popular reproach in connection with government measures which aroused opposition. During Adams's term he continued, in a sense, to fill this rôle, for it was believed, with some reason, that he "secretly ruled the cabinet of Mr. Adams."[161] The proposals of Hamilton at the time of the Convention were made public early in 1798 under the head, "IMPORTANT DOCUMENT," and with an editorial note declaring that it "completely unmasks the political character of the man who has been most instrumental in entailing on the United States those pernicious systems under which they now groan."[162] Hamilton was referred to quite commonly as "an avowed monarchist."[163] In a curious publication of 1799, professing to be a confidential letter from a monarchical Federalist, Hamilton was suggested as the founder of a royal dynasty for the United States. It was argued that an American monarchy might actually be instituted, despite the existing hostility to the idea, judging by the precedents of the acceptance of stamp duties, an excise tax, and, in Connecticut, an Episcopal bishop. "Let us look to the substance and adapt to it such terms as will be most palatable," ran the conclusion.[164] Hamilton's appointment as second in command (first

[158]Letter of May 26, 1792, Hamilton, *Works* (Lodge ed.), VIII, 264.
[159]Callender, *Seven Letters*, 5.
[160]Letter of Dec. 2, 1795, *American Historical Association Report, 1903*, II, 795.
[161]See, for example, the *Aurora*, Jan. 26, 1801, p. 2.
[162]*Ibid.*, Jan. 13, 1798, p. 3.
[163]For examples see *ibid.*, July 21, 1798, p. 3; *ibid.*, Feb. 5, 1801, p. 2.
[164]*Ibid.*, Mar. 2, 1799, p. 2.

under Washington) in the army raised against France in 1798[165] may have suggested this letter, for in it Hamilton is designated as "the great director of our plans, the real and not the ostensible commander of our military forces."

Other "monarchists"[166] could be listed and the charges against them reviewed, but it would add little of moment to the account presented. Certain conclusions are apparent from the charges against Washington, Adams, and Hamilton. Some of them may have been sincere expressions of a fear that the Executive would become so powerful as to be unseated or brought to terms by nothing short of revolution. But in most cases "monarchy" and "monarchical" were either abusive epithets, produced by the intense party feelings of the times, or were terms intended to call attention to alleged similarities between the federalists and real royalists.

In the century and more since the Jeffersonian democrats "saved the country from monarchy" similar charges have been by one party or another. One occasionly hears them to-day in the Senate chamber[167] or reads them in our periodicals.[168] But in drawing conclusions it must not be forgotten that in the last years of the eighteenth century the experiment of republican government was in a much less advanced stage than at the present time and that the absurdity of erecting a monarchy in the United States had not yet been entirely established.

[165]On the act increasing the army and similar Federalist "war measures" of 1798 see Bassett, *The Federalist System*, 237.

[166]Most notably Gouverneur Morris.

[167]See *Congressional Record*, 66th Congress, 2d Session, 3503, 4124-4129, 4683-4689.

[168]For examples see "Autocracy For The U. S. Real Menace After War," by John Temple Graves, in the *Chicago Examiner*, May 27, 1917. See Mr. Root's speech as temporary chairman of the New York Republican Convention, *New York Times*, Feb. 20, 1920. The *Chicago Tribune*, in its leading editorial, August 6, 1921, furnishes an especially clear-cut example of the use of such charges as applied to state politics.

CONCLUSION

Thomas Hart Benton, in his "Thirty Years' View," records some words of Rufus King with the comment that they "ought to be remembered by future generations, to enable them to appreciate justly those founders of our government who were in favor of a stronger organization than was adopted." They are as follows:

"You young men [Benton and his generation] who have been born since the Revolution, look with horror upon the name of a King, and upon all propositions for a strong government. It was not so with us. We were born the subjects of a King, and were accustomed to subscribe ourselves 'His Majesty's most faithful subjects'; and we began the quarrel which ended in the Revolution, not against the King, but against his parliament."[1]

This survey of American ideas on government from 1776 to 1801 has presented evidences of the attitude described by Rufus King. The survival of monarchical predilections appeared sufficiently persistent to lead men to give serious consideration to plans, or rumors of plans, of a monarchical nature. Yet if certain men of more than average ability and reputation considered such plans desirable and feasible they hesitated to publish them to the people. They welcomed the Constitution of 1787 with a show of relief which convinces one that if they had desired a monarchical government it was not as an end in itself but as a means of assuring security for "life, liberty and property."

The charges of monarchical purposes brought against the Federalist administrations were for the most part unjustified. Yet they can be understood as manifestations of sincere apprehension on the part of men not yet accustomed to the efficient operations of a strong central government. Party differences arising from the domestic situation were accentuated by the division of opinion

[1]T. H. Benton, *Thirty Years' View*, I, 58. Compare and contrast Jefferson's remark, March 15, 1789, quoted above, 56, and footnote on same page.

on contemporary affairs in Europe. The war between Great Britain and France loomed large in the eyes of Americans as a struggle between monarchy and democracy, or, in the terms of the day, between tyranny and anarchy. The outcome was an absence of mutual understanding and coöperation between parties in America, which resulted, in turn, in the exploitation of monarchical charges.

The caution and secrecy maintained in regard to monarchical plans by the persons most favorably inclined towards them, contrasted with the loud-voiced accusations of their political opponents, indicate the existence of popular aversion to monarchy in the period studied.

The main results of the study may be concisely summarized as follows:

I. There is reason to believe that several plans of monarchical character received serious consideration in the United States between 1776 and 1787.

II. The character of the men associated with them entitles these plans to considerable attention.

III. The existence of monarchical purposes in the Constitutional Convention is largely a matter of definition.

IV. The exigencies of practical politics after 1787 account for much but not all of the current suspicion regarding monarchical tendencies from 1787 to 1801.

V. Nearly all of the evidence observed reinforces the belief that the people of the United States were essentially antimonarchical in the period studied.

APPENDIX A

Colonel Nicola's Apologies to General Washington for having made to him certain Monarchical Propositions.

I

Fishkill 23 May 1782

Sr

I am this moment honoured with yours and am extremely unhappy that the liberty I have taken should be so highly disagreeable to your Excellency, tho I have met with a many severe misfortunes nothing has ever affected me so much as your reproof. I flatter myself no man is more desirous to be governed by the dictates of true religion and honour, & since I have erred I entreat you will attribute it more to weakness of judgment than corruptness of heart. No man has entered into the present dispute with more zeal, from a full conviction of the justness of it, & I look on every person who endeavours to disturb the repose of his country as a villain, if individuals disapprove of any thing in the form of government they live under they have no other choice but a proper submission or to retire. The scheme I mentioned did not appear to me in a light any way injurious to my country, rather likely to prove beneficial, but since I find your sentiment so different from mine I shall consider myself as having been under a strong delusion, & beg leave to assure you it shall be my future study to combate, as far as my abilities reach, every gleam of discontent. Excuse the confusion of this occasion by the distraction of my mind & permit me to subscribe myself with due respect

Your Excellenies

Most obedt Servant

Lewis Nicola Col. Inv.

II

Fishkill 24 May 1782

S[r]

Greatly oppressed in mind & distressed at having been the means of giving your Excellency one moments uneasiness, I find myself under the necessity of relying on your goodness to pardon my further troubling you by endeavouring, if possible, to remove every unfavourable impression that lies in your breast to my prejudice. Alway anxious to stand fair in the opinion of good men the idea of your thinking me capable of acting or abetting any villainy must make me very unhappy.

I solemnly assure your Excellency I have neither been the broacher, or in any shape the encourager of the design not to seperate at the peace 'till all grievances are redressed, but have often heard it mentioned either directly or by hints.

From sundry resolves of Congress favourable to the army, but which that Hon[b]. Body has not been able to execute, persons who only see what swims on the surface have laid the blame at their door & therefore lost all confidence in promises, how far this bad impression may affect the larger part of the army I cannot say, but should it operate considerably at the conclusion of the war, it may be expected that all obligations shall be immediately discharged, the possibility of which I much doubt, therefore I took the liberty of mentioning what I thought would be a compromise, bidding fair to be satisfactory to one side and not disadvantageous to the other.

Deprived by misfortunes of that patrimony I was born to, and with a numerous family, depending entirely upon my military appointments, when these have failed the tender feelings of a husband and father, seeing his family often destitute of the common necessaries of life, have pierced my soul, these feelings often repeated & fraught with anxiety for the future may have sowered my mind & warped my judgment, but in the most sacred manner I protest that had I influence & abilities equal to the task the idea of occasioning any commotions in a country I lived in would be daggers in my breast, and I should think myself accountable at the grand tribunal for all the mischiefs that might ensue, was it my fate to live under a government I thought insupportable I would look on retiring to some other as the only justifiable means I could pursue.

As to my opinion on different forms of government, if it be erroneous, I assure you the fault is owing to a defect in judgment not a willful shutting my eyes to the light of reason.

However wrong the sentiments I have disclosed to your Excellency may be, they cannot have done any mischief, as they have always remained locked up in my breast.

My mind was so disturbed at the perusal of your Excellencies letter that I do not know what answer I returned, if there was any thing improper in it I must trust to your humanity for pardon & request you will believe me with unfeigned respect

S[r]

Your Excellencies most obed[t] Servant
Lewis Nicola Col Inv.

III

Fishkill 28 Febr[y] 1782 ["Ought to be 28th May 1782" according to Washington's endorsement]

S[r]

Since I was honoured with your Excellencies Letter of the 22d Inst. I have assiduously endeavoured to recollect, not only each paragraph, but also every expression of that ill fated representation which has been the occasion of so much trouble to you & anxiety to me, in order to find out what could occasion my intentions being so greatly misapprehended, and cannot attribute it to any thing but an inability to express my sentiments with sufficient pespicuity, and its being introduced by complaints that apparently bear hard on & censure the supreme authority of our Union, which so prejudiced your mind as to prevent attention to my request, that your Excell[cy] would judge of the whole together & not by detached parts. From this consideration I am induced to trespass further on your goodness in hopes of putting them in a clearer point of view.

Far has it been from my thoughts to suppose that Congress ever entered into an engagement, or made a promise they did not intend to fullfil, but as they were not always executed, I endeavoured to find out the true cause, and by considering such circumstances as have come to my knowledge concluded they were prevented, in some cases by the untoward circumstances of the times, and in others, by the contracted [?] principles of some without whose assistance that Hon.[b] Body cannot perform them. I could mention several things in support of this opinion but shall only trouble your Excellency with one report I have heard since my return here, which is that some of the eastern States refused to comply with the request of Congress, to be allowed a duty of 5 per cent on imported goods, from the consideration that if it had such a fund it would be enabled to pay the half pay to the officers already reformed. How true this is is, is impossible for me to determine, but supposing it otherwise, if believed it may operate as much as if it were gospel.

Tho I do not pretend to a larger portion of understanding than the generallity of mankind, yet I flatter myself I am neither an idiot or crazed, one or the other of which must have been the case had I singled out your Excellency for the purpose of countenancing mutiny or treason, & as a fit person to unbosom myself preferably to every other individual within my reach; this I hope will be sufficient to clear me from every suspicion of harbouring sinister designs, and that however inaptly I may have expressed myself, my intention was not to promote but, as far as in me lay, prevent designs that may some time or other be carried into execution & occasion great mischief.

My apprehensions were founded on the following considerations. That numbers of our privates are dissatisfied & ready to break out, were they not prevented by the virtue of their officers, were any number of the latter, at the peace, to consider themselves in danger of being deprived of the fruits of their toils & hazards; of the reward of their services, on which several may depend for the future support of themselves & families, & join with the men the consequence may be fatal; Impressed by these ideas I know not to what man or body of men I could better address myself than to your Excellency, as I am persuaded none is more enabled, by influence on the army, to counter act any bad designs. No person can be more interested in Congress's fulfilling all her engagements than I am, yet I flatter myself that will be done voluntarily or obtained by justifiable means.

Tho the above was a main-consideration I must own it was not the only one, but that I was prompted to the step I took by another inducement. The different forms of gove.[t] under which men live, or have lived, have frequently employed my most serious thoughts and the conclusion that all, the jewish Theocracy excepted, have many defects accompanying their good qualities, & that if the latter could be culled & formed into one system it would bid fair to be the most perfect human art could device. When we assumed independence, & each state formed a plan of government for itself I was astonished that none of the thirteen had adopted the english Constitution purged of its defects till I considered that reformers seldom hit the true point of rest, but never stop 'till they reach, one diametrically opposite to that they set out from without considering that extremes may be equally vicious. Montesquieu observes that warm climates are best adapted to subjection & cold ones to freedom, but his sagacity could not foresee that the inhabitants of the sultry climate of Georgia as well as those of the cold region of the Province of Main would have both concurred in rejecting every shaddow of Monarchy.

A man of 60 years of age may reasonably expect that a young republican government will not, in his time, be so vitiated as to render living under it intolerable, therefore, had I none to regard but myself, I should endeavour to glide through the dregs of life with tranquillity, but as my many children give me a prospect of a numerous issue I wish to leave them with the fairest prospect of political felicity possible, therefore as soon as Congress & some States promised to reward their troops with lands I could not help forming the pleasing hopes they might be induced to allot them contiguous to each, with liberty of forming a distinct State under such form of government as those that chose to emigrate might prefer. Satsified that no person is more likely, by interest with Congress & influence with the army, to promote such a scheme, if approved of, than your Excellency, I took the liberty fully to describe my thoughts to you, & to you allone, possibly induced by the pleasing hopes of seeing a favorite project realised, to go too far.

In such a project as mine the utmost attention should [be] had to every stone of the foundation, which should not be laid without mature deliberation, & that under the guidance of a person who, to considerable abilities can add such a rectitude of heart as to prefer the publick weal to all the dazling prospects of prerogative

I fear words cannot be sufficient to appologise for the great liberty I have taken therefore shall not trespas any farther on your lenity than to assure you that I am with great respect

S[r]

Your Excellencies

Most obed[t] Servant,

Lewis Nicola Col. Inv.

APPENDIX B

BIBLIOGRAPHY

I. Source Material

1. *Documents and Contemporary Writings*

John Adams, *Works*. Edited by C. F. Adams. 9 vols. Boston, 1850–1856. The *Works* form volumes II-X of C. F. Adams's *Life and Works of John Adams*. In some respects the most valuable collection used, because of the writer's importance throughout the period, and because of the frankness with which he reveals his reaction to the political changes of his time.

John Quincy Adams, *Memoirs*. Edited by C. F. Adams. 12 vols. Philadelphia, 1874–1877. Of importance to the present study rather for what it omits than what it includes.

Samuel Adams, *Writings*. Edited by H. A. Cushing. 4 vols. New York, 1904–1908. Especially helpful for the early period, when it reveals, in part, the colonial attitude towards the British monarchical government.

American Antiquarian Society Proceedings, new series, XV. Worcester, 1904. Includes material on the Shays Rebellion.

American Archives. Compiled under authority of Congress by Peter Force. 9 vols. Washington, 1837–1853. Contains a wealth of material (legislative acts, speeches, *et cetera* for 1774–1776) which is difficult of access because awkwardly arranged.

American Historical Review. New York, 1895—. Includes source material such as James Wilkinson's oath of allegiance to Spain and correspondence between Ira Allen and British officials.

Annals of the Congress of the United States (1789–1824). 42 vols. Washington, 1834–1856.

Belknap Papers (*Massachusetts Historical Society Collections*, 5th ser., II, III; 6th ser., IV). Boston, 1877 and 1891. Cover years 1766–1798, but the greater number of letters were written after 1780. The Belknap-Hazard group are of special interest as revealing the interests of conservatives of the years 1779–1788.

Phineas Bond, *Letters* (*American Historical Association Report, 1896*, I, 513–659). Edited by J. Franklin Jameson. British consular reports for 1787–1789. Betrays no undue interest in American political arrangements.

Marquis de Bouillé, *Souvenirs and Fragments.* (Published as part of a series by "La Société d'Histoire Contemporaine.") Paris, 1906–1911. The author was a personal friend of Prince Henry of Prussia, and described him at some length.

Bowdoin and Temple Papers (*Massachusetts Historical Society Collections*, 7th ser., VI). Boston, 1907. Covers the years 1783–1809. Includes a letter to Gorham in 1786.

Aedanus Burke, *Considerations on the Society of Cincinnati.* Hartford [1783?] (There was also a Philadelphia edition, 1783.) A pamphlet which proved effective in arousing hostility to the society as creating "a race of hereditary patricians, or nobility."

J. T. Callender, *The Prospect Before Us.* Richmond, 1800. A violent campaign pamphlet, based in part on the writer's observations, as a visitor, in the house of representatives "for the greater part of five sessions." Asserts the Federalists are "monarchists."

J. T. Callender, (reputed author), *Seven Letters to Alexander Hamilton, King of the Feds.* New York, 1802. Appears separately, also in *Duane's Pamphlets*, New York, 1814. Thought by W. C. Ford to be wrongly accredited to J. T. Callendar, since he had left the Anti-Federalist ranks by 1802. Ridicules Hamilton for his attack on Adams. Calls Hamilton the "greatest Machiavel in America," and denounces the Federalists generally.

Reports on Canadian Archives, 1889–1890. By Douglas Brymner, Archivist. Ottawa, 1890, 1891. Very valuable, especially for its presentation of contemporary evidence on Canadian-American relations.

Marquis de Chastellux, *Travels in North America in 1780, 1781, and 1782. Translated from the French by an English gentleman, who resided in America at that period. With notes by the translator.* 2 vols. London, 1787. By far the best commentary on

American political developments of any of the travellers' accounts of the times, so far as the present writer has found. The Marquis was impressed with the devotion of the people to Washington, by the reaction against English forms of government, *et cetera.*

WILLIAM COBBETT, *Political Works.* Edited by J. M. and J. P. Cobbett. 6 vols. London, preface dated 1835. As a vigorous exponent of the British monarchy and at the same time a supporter of the American Federalist party Cobbett ("Peter Porcupine") seemed to the Anti-Federalists a living example of the union of Federalism and monarchism.

Congressional Record, Containing the Proceedings and Debates. Washington, 1873 to date. Used for February and March, 1920.

Journals of the Continental Congress. Edited by W. C. Ford and Gaillard Hunt. 23 vols. to date. Washington, 1904—. Madison's "Notes of Debates" appear for 1782–1783. The volumes for 1783 are in preparation.

TENCH COXE, *An Examination of the Constitution for the United States of America of America, Submitted to the People by the General Convention, at Philadelphia, the 17th. Day of September, 1787, and Since Adopted and Ratified by the Conventions of Eleven States, Chosen for the Purpose of Considering It, Being all that have yet Decided on the Subject.* Philadelphia, 1788. Points out the "safety of the people, from the restraints imposed on the President" and from other excellent features of the Constitution.

TENCH COXE, *Strictures upon the Letter imputed to Mr. Jefferson addressed to Mr. Mazzei.* 1800. His main object is to prove that the sentiments and observations of the letter are correct.

Manasseh Cutler, *Life, Journals, and Correspondence.* Edited by W. P. and J. P. Cutler. 2 vols. Cincinnati, 1888.

Silas Deane, *Papers* (*New York Historical Society Collections,* XIX-XXIII). Edited by Charles Isham, New York, 1887–1891. The papers cover the years 1774–1790.

JOHN DICKINSON, *Writings* (*Memoirs of the Historical Society of Pennsylvania,* XIV). Edited by P. L. Ford. Philadelphia, 1895. Valuable for the early part of the period when Dickinson's writings were a power throughout the country.

Documents Relating to New England Federalism, 1800-1815. Edited by Henry Adams. Boston, 1877. Of interest in the present study as depicting the political aftermath of the "republican triumph."

J. ELLIOT, compiler, *Debates in the Several State Conventions, on the Adoption of the Federal Constitution . . .* 5 vols. Philadelphia and Washington, 1866.

Essex Institute Historical Collections, XXV. Salem, 1899.

MAX FARRAND, editor, *Records of the Federal Convention of 1787. . . .* 3 vols. New Haven, 1911. Contains the official journal, the quasi-official records by Madison, and the notes of certain other delegates, together with much other data, such as statements on the Convention by various members. An excellent index is a feature of the work.

The Federalist, a Commentary on the Constitution . . . by Alexander Hamilton, James Madison, and John Jay. Edited by P. L. Ford. New York, copyrighted 1898.

BENJAMIN FRANKLIN, *Writings.* Edited by A. H. Smyth. 10 vols. New York, 1905–1907.

ALBERT GALLATIN, *Writings.* Edited by Henry Adams. 3 vols. Philadelphia, 1879. Worthy of note for their very indifference to the "monarchical" charges which so many men of Gallatin's party were bringing against the Federalists.

ALEXANDER HAMILTON, *Works.* Edited by J. C. Hamilton. 7 vols. New York, 1850–1851.

ALEXANDER HAMILTON, *Works.* Edited by H. C. Lodge. 9 vols. New York, 1885–1886. A more complete edition than that by J. C. Hamilton. The correspondence is especially valuable to the present study.

ALEXANDER HAMILTON, *Works.* Federal edition. Edited by H. C. Lodge. 12 vols. New York and London, 1904.

PATRICK HENRY, *Life, Correspondence and Speeches.* Edited by W. W. Henry. 3 vols. New York, 1891. Represents the extreme antimonarchical attitude in the early part of the period.

C. HIPPEAU, *Le Gouvernement de Normandie au XVIIe et XVIIIe Siècle*, III. Caen, 1864. Includes letters from America by St. John de Crèvecoeur.

WILLIAM HULL, *An Oration Delivered to the Society of the Cincinnati in the Commonwealth of Massachusetts, July 4, 1788.* Boston, 1788. Reviews the political situation from the eve of the Revolution to midsummer 1788.

The Life and Times of David Humphreys, by F. L. Humphreys. 2 vols. New York and London, 1917. Worthy of note as source material because of the large amount of correspondence included.

GAILLARD HUNT And JAMES BROWN SCOTT, editors, *The Debates in the Federal Convention of 1787 Which Framed the Constitution of the United States of America, Reported by James Madison a Delegate from the State of Virginia.* International edition. New York (Oxford University Press), 1920. This edition of the *Debates* is in some respects an improvement upon that by Farrand but, on the whole, less helpful to the present study. The more important quotations above have been checked with the newer edition but only minor differences have been found.

JOHN JAY, *Correspondence and Public Papers*. Edited by H. P. Johnston. 4 vols. New York, 1890–1893. Especially suggestive of the reaction of conservative persons to the disorders of 1786.

THOMAS JEFFERSON, *Writings*. Edited by H. A. Washington. 9 vols. Washington, 1853–1854. Sometimes called "Congress Edition."

THOMAS JEFFERSON, *Writings*. Edited by P. L. Ford. 10 vols. New York, 1892–1899.

Journal, Acts and Proceedings, of the Convention . . . Which Formed the Constitution of the United States. Published in conformity to a Resolution of Congress. Boston, 1819.

The Life of John Kalb, by Friedrick Kapp. English translation. New York, 1870. Contains some valuable letters and reports.

The Life and Correspondence of Rufus King. Edited by C. R. King. 6 vols. New York, 1894–1900. Includes many letters illustrating the political views of this important Federalist.

The Life and Correspondence of Henry Knox, by F. S. Drake. Boston, 1873. Contains a number of letters helpful to the present study.

CHARLES LEE, *Papers* (*New York Historical Society Collections*, IV-VII). New York, 1871–1874. Vivid but very partisan commentaries on men and issues of the day.

RICHARD HENRY LEE, *Letters*. Edited by J. C. Ballagh. 2 vols. New York, 1911–1914. Covers nearly the entire period and somewhat balances the impressions one gets from Federalist writings.

WILLIAM MACDONALD, editor, *Select Charters and Other Documents Illustrative of American History, 1606–1775.* New York, 1910.

WILLIAM MACLAY, *Journal.* Edited by E. S. Maclay. New York, 1890. An intimate account of the organization of the government under the present Constitution, full of gibes at "monarchical tendencies."

JAMES MADISON, *Papers.* Edited by H. D. Gilpin. 3 vols. Washington, 1840.

JAMES MADISON, *Writings.* Edited by Gaillard Hunt. 9 vols. New York, 1900–1910.

The Magazine of History, XXIII. New York and Poughkeepsie, 1916. Prints a letter by J. M. Varnum.

Massachusetts Historical Society Proceedings. 52 vols. Boston and Cambridge, 1794–1919. Include much scattered source material, such as extracts from correspondence and journals. (Items under the *Collections* of the Society form entire volumes and are listed under their special titles.)

G. R. MINOT, *History of the Insurrections in Massachusetts.* Boston, 1788 and 1810. An historical account by a Massachusetts man of the time. Breathes a spirit of reconciliation.

Michigan Pioneer and Historical Collections, XXIV, Lansing, 1895. Prints interesting contemporary comments by Canadians on political tendencies in the United States.

JAMES MONROE, *Writings.* Edited by S. M. Hamilton. 7 vols. New York, 1898–1903. Contain few references to "monarchists."

H. NILES, editor, *Principles and Acts of the Revolution.* Baltimore, 1822. An old but rather useful collection of sources.

Records of the Ohio Company, edited by A. B. Hulbert; see below, II, 2.

THOMAS PAINE, *Writings.* Edited by M. D. Conway. 4 vols. New York, 1894–1896. The best collection of Paine's works.

THOMAS POWNALL, *The Administration of the British Colonies*, 5th edition. 2 vols. London, 1774. A thoughtful work by a former colonial governor. Desires imperial reorganization to restore harmony.

JOHN ROWE, *Diary* (*Massachusetts Historical Society Proceedings*, 2d ser., X, 11-108). An interesting account of events in Massachusetts, 1764–1779, by a conservative Boston merchant.

ARTHUR ST. CLAIR, *Papers*. Edited by W. H. Smith. 2 vols. Cincinnati, 1882. Of importance as revealing the political ideas of a prominent revolutionary general and statesman.

JAMES BROWN SCOTT, co-editor, *The Debates in the Federal Convention . . . Reported by James Madison . . .* Listed above under Gaillard Hunt.

Life and Correspondence of Samuel Seabury. By E. E. Beardsley. Boston, 1881. Less important to a political than a religious study.

Spurious Letters of Washington. Edited by W. C. Ford. Brooklyn, 1889. These "Letters" were dated as written in the earlier months of the Revolution, and were published to injure Washington at the time of the Jay treaty agitation. They represented him as never really renouncing loyalty to the royal government.

B. F. STEVENS, *Facsimiles of Manuscripts in European Archives relating to America, 1773–1783*. 24 portfolios. 1889–1895, index, 1898. Of interest in the present connection for certain papers bearing on the De Broglie ambitions.

EZRA STILES, *Literary Diary*. Edited by F. B. Dexter. 3 vols. New York, 1901. Contains many comments on public affairs.

J. G. SWIFT, *Memoirs*, 1890. Swift was a confidential friend of President Monroe and recorded the latter's reference to Nathaniel Gorham's supposed letter to Prince Henry.

DR. THACHER, *Sermon on the Death of Nathaniel Gorham*. [Boston], 1796. Contains some references to Gorham's life and character.

Vermont Historical Society Collections. 2 vols. Montpelier, 1870, 1871. Contains valuable source material on the negotiations between Vermont and Canada.

Warren-Adams Letters, 1743–1777 (*Massachusetts Historical Society Collections*, LXXII). Boston, 1917. Some interesting letters by John Adams, written in confidential vein, are a feature of the collection.

GEORGE WASHINGTON, *Writings*. Edited by J. Sparks. 12 vols. Boston, 1837.

GEORGE WASHINGTON, *Writings*. Edited by W. C. Ford. 14 vols. New York, 1889.

DR. WELSH, *Eulogy to the Memory of Nathaniel Gorham*. Boston, 1796. The most complete account of Gorham that appears to exist.

FRANCIS WHARTON, *The Revolutionary Diplomatic Correspondence of the United States.* 6 vols. Washington, 1889.

2. *Manuscripts*

(With one exception, that of the Crèvecoeur Letter of July 22, 1787, the manuscripts listed are in the Manuscripts Division of the Library of Congress.)

American Stamp Act Collection. Of heterogeneous character, including such items as an anonymous diary for 1765–1770 (apparently by Ebenezer Hazard) and contemporary prints caricaturing the ministry.

WILLIAM ARMSTRONG, *Papers, 1762–1814.* Transcripts. For the most part of little or no value for the present study, but cited in one case.

Continental Congress, Papers, Letter Books of the Presidents, May 28, 1781–Aug. 9, 1787. 1 vol. The letters of Nathaniel Gorham as President (as well as those of John Hancock) are conspicuous by their absence.

HECTOR ST. JEAN DE CRÈVECOEUR, *Letter to William Short,* July 22, 1787. Original in the Library of the Historical Society of Pennsylvania. Described above, in chapter IV.

NATHAN DANE, *Letters.* Twenty in number, written between 1785 and 1814, some by Dane but more to him. Extremely interesting for their failure to harmonize with the conception that the years 1785–1787 were so obviously critical as to drive men in despair to frame a new constitution. They deserve special study and interpretation.

BENJAMIN FRANKLIN, *Miscellaneous Papers.* Contain some correspondence with Nathaniel Gorham.

JAMES MADISON, *Notes on Debates in the Continental Congress, 1782–1783, 1787.* Sixteen little volumes that give the reader a more vivid picture of the disputes and difficulties of the Continental Congress than otherwise available. (They have been published in various works.) They furnish one of the few sources for an understanding of Nathaniel Gorham.

JAMES MADISON, *Papers,* 105 vols. Only special items, reached through the *Calendar,* were examined by the present writer.

JAMES MONROE, *Papers,* 22 vols. Examined as in case of Madison *Papers.*

LEWIS NICOLA, *Propositions to Washington and Apologies.* See above, Chapter III, and Appendix A.

A Collection of Letters Written to and by William Plumer and Transcribed for his Amusement and Instruction. Covers the years 1781–1804. Especially interesting as showing some of the origins of his later Federalist sympathies.

THOMAS RODNEY, *Diary.* Contains character sketches of his colleagues in Congress in 1781, and later comments on public events after his retirement to private life. The writer was a brother to Caesar Rodney. The *Diary* betrays an unbalanced mental state.

WILLIAM SHORT, *Papers.* A remarkable collection of 52 volumes, for 1778–1849, 31 of which are within the period of the present study. Short, for many years in Europe, both in private and official capacity, corresponded with a variety of persons, from Thomas Paine to Alexander Hamilton, and on both European and American affairs.

Stamp Act Congress Collection. Similar to *American Stamp Act Collection.*

EZRA STILES, *Literary Diary, 1770–1790.* Force Transcripts. Contains some passages omitted from the printed edition.

HENRY TAZEWELL, *Twelve Letters, 1796–1798.* Tazewell was a member of Congress from Virginia. His letters are long and full of comments on public affairs.

GEORGE WASHINGTON, *Papers,* especially vols. 198 and 200. Examined especially for correspondence with Nicola and Varnum.

3. *Newspapers*

The Newport Mercury; or The Weekly Advertiser. Newport (R. I.), 1758–. Photographic facsimiles for 1766–1776 used for the present study. By its exchange articles from other papers it affords a broader view than its place of publication may suggest. It is, in a way, a repertory of sources, for it brings together a large number of addresses, petitions, resolutions, and the like. More important, it presents them to us in the form and context in which they were presented to the reading public of 1766–1776.

Newspaper Extracts, 1776–1780; *New Jersey Archives* (or, *Documents Relating to the Revolutionary History of the State of New Jersey*), 2d ser. I-IV. Paterson and Trenton, 1901–1914. Relate particularly to New Jersey but appear generally representative of the period. Little assistance to the present study due to confusion of monarchical with war issues.

Pennsylvania Packet and the General Advertiser, 1771–1790 (?); w., s. w., t. w., and 1784– daily.Philadelphia. Numbers for 1786 1788 examined. More news items and less controversial matter than the *Mercury*, or, later, the *Aurora*. Frankly interested in events in royal circles abroad. Expressed great admiration for Washington, on the eve of the Federal Convention. Supported the movement for an improved constitution.

Gazette of the United States and Daily Advertiser, 1794–1795. Philadelphia. Existed earlier and later under similar names. Founded in New York. John Fenno the editor. A "Hamiltonian" organ. Numbers for 1794 examined. Revealed support of strong and centralized government but no monarchical tendencies.

Aurora and General Advertiser (titles varied but these the chief ones), 1792 (?)-1826 (?); d. Philadelphia. Examined for 1797–1801. The most prominent newspaper of its time in the United States. Violently anti-administration, anti-British, and pro-French. Whatever the basis of its attacks the form in which they were made was frequently disgraceful. Very valuable for purposes for the present study.

New York Times, 1851-; d. New York. A single issue cited.

II. Secondary Material

1. *General Works*

a. *Bibliographical Aids*

Calendar of the Papers of Benjamin Franklin in the Library of the American Philosophical Society. Edited by I. M. Hays. 5 vols. Philadelphia, 1908. (See below, *List of the . . . Franklin Papers*.)

Calendar of the Correspondence of James Madison (*Bureau of Rolls and Library of the Department of State*, no. 4). Washington, March, 1894.

Calendar of Monroe Papers. (See above, James Monroe, *Papers*).

Calendar of Washington Manuscripts in the Library of Congress. Prepared by Herbert Friedenwald. Washington, 1901.

Calendar of the Correspondence of George Washington with the Continental Congress. Prepared by J. C. Fitzpatrick. Washington, 1906.

Calendar of the Correspondence of George Washington Commander in Chief of the Continental Army with the Officers. Prepared by J. C. Fitzpatrick. 4 vols. Washington, 1915.

E. Channing, A. B. Hart, and F. J. Turner, editors, *Guide to the Study and Reading of American History.* Boston and London, 1914.

Check List of American Newspapers in the Library of Congress. Prepared by A. B. Slauson, Washington, 1901.

Check List of Personal Papers in Historical Societies . . . and other Learned Institutions in the United States. Compiled by J. C. Fitzpatrick. Washington, 1918.

Handbook of Manuscripts in the Library of Congress. Compiled by Gaillard Hunt and others. Washington, 1918.

J. N. Larned, editor. *The Literature of American History.* Boston, 1902.

List of the Benjamin Franklin Papers in the Library of Congress. Edited by W. C. Ford. Washington, 1905.

James Monroe *Papers, Listed in Chronological Order from the . . . Manuscripts in the Library of Congress.* Compiled by W. C. Ford. Washington, 1904.

b. *Encyclopedic Aids*

American Historical Association, Index to Papers and Annual Reports, 1884-1914 (American Historical Association Reports, 1914, II). Compiled by D. M. Matteson. Washington, 1918.

Appletons' Cyclopaedia of American Biography. Edited by J. G. Wilson and John Fiske. 7 vols. New York, 1900.

Biographical Congressional Directory, 1774–1911 (Senate Documents, vol. 56, 61st Congress, 2d session). Washington, 1913.

Encyclopaedia Britannica, 11th edition. 29 vols. Cambridge and New York, 1910–1911.

Jeffersonian Cyclopedia . . . . Edited by John P. Foley. New York and London, 1900. Very helpful to a study of the present nature.

Lamb, *Biographical Dictionary of the United States.* Edited by J. H. Brown. 7 vols. Boston, 1900-1903.

Pierre Larousse, *Grand Dictionnaire Universel Français.* 15 vols. 1866–1890.

National Encyclopaedia of American Biography. 15 vols. New York, 1898–1916.

New International Encyclopaedia, 2d edition. 23 vols. New York, 1914–1916.

c. *General Historical Accounts*

HENRY ADAMS, *History of the United States*. 9 vols. New York, 1889–1891.

American Historical Association Papers. 5 vols. New York, 1886–1891.

American Historical Association Reports, 1890–1916. Washington, 1890–1919.

GEORGE BANCROFT, *History of the Formation of the Constitution*, 2 vols. New York, 1882.

J. S. BASSETT, *A Short History of the United States*. New York, 1914.

C. L. BECKER, *Beginnings of the American People* (The Riverside History of the United States, I). Boston and New York, 1915.

EDWARD CHANNING, *A History of the United States*. 4 vols. New York and London, 1907–1917.

G. T. CURTIS, *Constitutional History of the United States*. 2 vols. New York, 1889-1902. Volume I a reprint from the author's *History of the Constitution*, 1854. Volume II is edited by J. C. Clayton.

RICHARD FROTHINGHAM, *Rise of the Republic of the United States*. Boston, 1872.

J. C. HAMILTON, *History of the Republic of the United States of America, as Traced in the Writings of Alexander Hamilton*. 7 vols. New York, 1857.

RICHARD HILDRETH, *History of the United States*. 6 vols. New York, 1849–1856.

H. E. VON HOLST, *Constitutional and Political History of the United States*. Translated by J. J. Lalor. 8 vols. Chicago, 1879–1892.

J. B. MCMASTER, *A History of the People of the United States*. 8 vols. New York and London, 1884–1913.

JUSTIN WINSOR, *Narrative and Critical History of America* Boston and New York. 8 vols. Copyrighted, 1889.

2. *Works on Special Subjects*

C. F. ADAMS, *Life of John Adams* (volume I of *Life and Works of John Adams*). Boston, 1856.

J. S. BASSETT, *The Federalist System* (*The American Nation: A History*, XI). New York and London, 1906.

C. A. BEARD, *An Economic Interpretation of the Constitution of the United States*. New York, 1913.

C. A. BEARD, *Economic Origins of Jeffersonian Democracy*. New York, 1915.

E. E. BEARDSLEY, *Life and Correspondence of Samuel Seabury*. 2d edition. Boston, 1881.

S. F. BEMIS, "The Vermont Separatists and Great Britain" (*American Historical Review*, XXI, 547-560).

T. H. BENTON, *Thirty Years View . . . of the American Government . . . from 1820-1850*. 2 vols. New York, 1856–1858.

A. J. BEVERIDGE, *The Life of John Marshall*. 2 vols. Boston and New York, 1916.

MARIA CAMPBELL, *Revolutionary Services and Civil Life of General William Hull*. New York and Philadelphia, 1848.

M. D. CONWAY, *Omitted Chapters of History Disclosed in the Life and Papers of Edmund Randolph*. 2d edition. New York, 1889.

W. S. CULBERTSON, *Essay on Alexander Hamilton*. New Haven and London, 1911.

W. P. and J. P. CUTLER, *Life, Journals, and Correspondence of Manasseh Cutler, L.L.D.* 2 vols. Cincinnati, 1888.

HENRI DONIOL, *Histoire de la Participation de la France à l'Établissement des États-Unis d'Amérique*. 5 vols., Paris, 1886–1892. Complément du tome V, 1899.

F. S. Drake, *Life and Correspondence of Henry Knox*. Boston, 1883.

F. S. DRAKE, *Memorials of the Society of the Cincinnati of Massachusetts*. Boston, 1873.

MAX FARRAND, *Framing of the Constitution*. New Haven, 1913.

JOHN FISKE, *The Critical Period of American History, 1783-1789*. 5th edition. Boston and New York, 1889.

W. C. FORD, "Manuscripts and Historical Archives" (*American Historical Association Report, 1913*, i, 75-84.)

W. C. FORD, *The Spurious Letters of Washington.* Brooklyn, 1889.

T. M. GREEN, *The Spanish Conspiracy,* Cincinnati, 1891.

B. H. HALL, *History of Eastern Vermont.* New York, 1858.

C. D. HAZEN, "The French Revolution as Seen by the Americans of the Eighteenth Century" (*American Historical Association Report, 1895,* 455-466).

J. L. HEATON, *The Story of Vermont.* Boston, copyrighted, 1889.

S. P. HILDRETH, *Pioneer History . . . of the Northwest Territory.* Cincinnati and New York. 1848.

F. W. HOLDEN, "The Vermont of the Revolution" (*The Magazine of History,* XXII, 38-48; New York and Poughkeepsie, 1916).

G. E. HOWARD, *Preliminaries of the Revolution, 1763-1775* (*The American Nation: A History,* VIII). New York and London, 1905.

GAILLARD HUNT, "The President of the United States" (*Wisconsin Historical Publications,* LXIII, 76-98).

A. B. HULBERT, *Pioneers of the Republic.* Chicago, 1906.

A. B. HULBERT, editor, *Records of the Ohio Company* (*Marietta College Historical Collections,* I-III). Marietta, 1917.

F. L. HUMPHREYS, *Life and Times of David Humphreys.* 2 vols. New York and London, 1917.

CHARLES ISHAM, "A Short Account of the Life and Times of Silas Deane" (*American Historical Association Papers,* III, 41-47). New York and London, 1889.

"Journal of a French Traveller in the Colonies, 1765" (Documents) (*American Historical Review,* XXVI, 726-747; XXVII, 70-89).

FRIEDRICH KAPP, *Life of John Kalb.* New York, 1870.

FRIEDERICH KAPP, *Life of Frederick William Von Steuben.* New York, 1859.

RICHARD KRAUEL, "Prince Henry of Prussia and the Regency of the United States, 1786" (*American Historical Review,* October, 1911, 44-51.) London, 1912.

H. C. LODGE, *Alexander Hamilton* (*American Statesmen Series*). Boston, 1896.

A. C. MCLAUGHLIN, *The Confederation and the Constitution,* 1783-1789 (*The American Nation: A History,* X). New York and London, 1905.

R. M. MCELROY, *Kentucky in the Nation's History.* New York, 1909.

HUMPHREY MARSHALL, *The History of Kentucky*. 2d edition. 2 vols. Frankfort, 1824.

G. R. MINOT, *History of the Insurrections in Massachusetts*. Boston, 1788; 2d edition, 1810.

JULIA P. MITCHELL, *St. Jean de Crèvecoeur*. New York, 1916.

A. E. MORSE, *The Federalist Party in Massachusetts to the Year 1800*. Princeton, 1909.

F. S. OLIVER, *Alexander Hamilton; an Essay on American Union*. "New edition." London, 1907.

WILLIAM PLUMER, JR., *Life of William Plumer*. Boston, 1857.

C. A. W. POWNALL, *Life of Thomas Pownall*. London, copyrighted 1908.

C. J. RIETHMÜLLER, *Alexander Hamilton and His Contemporaries; or, the Rise of the American Constitution*. London, 1864. A little known life of Hamilton by an Englishman who connects Hamilton with his own devotion to the British monarchy.

A. E. RYERSON, *The Loyalists of America and Their Times*. 2d. edition. 2 vols. Toronto, 1880.

N. S. SHALER, *Kentucky: a Pioneer Commonwealth* (*American Commonwealth Series*). Boston, *osed*.

C. J. STILLÉ, "Comte de Broglie, the Proposed Stadtholder of America" (*Pennsylvania Magazine of History*, XI, 369-505). Philadelphia, 1887.

C. J. STILLÉ, *Life and Times of John Dickinson* (*Memoirs of the Historical Society of Pennsylvania*, XIII). Philadelphia, 1891.

M. C. TYLER, *Literary History of the American Revolution, 1763-1783*. 2 vols. New York, 1897.

C. H. VAN TYNE, *The American Revolution, 1776-1783* (*The American Nation: A History*, IX). New York and London, 1905.

C. H. VAN TYNE, "The Influence of the Clergy . . . in the American Revolution" (*American Historical Review*, XIX, 44-64). London, 1914.

C. M. WALSH, *The Political Science of John Adams*. New York and London, 1915.

SAMUEL WILLIAMS, *The Natural and Civil History of Vermont*, 2d. edition. 2 vols. Burlington, 1809.

MARGARET WOODBURY, *Public Opinion in Philadelphia, 1789-1801* (*Smith College Studies in History*, vol. V, nos. 1-2). Northampton, 1920.

INDEX